SNAP REVISION

READING

FOR UNDERSTANDING, ANALYSIS AND EVALUATION

For National 5 and Higher English

REVISE
FOR YOUR
SQA EXAMS

David Cockburn

Contents

Introduction

The Reading for Understanding, Analysis and Evaluation paper is one component of the N5 and Higher English assessment. It contributes 30% of the total marks available to your final marks.

The Reading for Understanding, Analysis and Evaluation paper assesses your ability to apply your reading skills to unseen material in a limited time. The passages for the Reading for Understanding, Analysis and Evaluation papers are often taken from quality newspapers and magazines, such as the *Herald*, *Scotsman*, *Guardian*, *Telegraph* and *Times*. You should try to read articles from such sources weekly. Quality newspapers are available online (you may need to register online). Throughout your courses, you should try to read at least one extended article each week, especially one that captures or widens your interests.

Many candidates are let down by a lack of vocabulary. To help overcome this, use a notebook or a memo app to make a note of unfamiliar words you find in your reading, and use a dictionary (or dictionary app) to find the meaning of the unfamiliar words. Do this regularly – you must extend and improve your vocabulary.

The N5 exam uses a single long passage. The Higher exam uses two passages, and questions may be asked about each one of the passages and about comparisons between the two passages.

Everything you learn about language for the Reading for Understanding, Analysis and Evaluation paper will help you perform better in the Critical Reading paper, where language questions require a similar approach.

How this book will help you

This book is written for both the National 5 and Higher levels. Most of the material covered is appropriate for both syllabuses. Work that is only appropriate for National 5 students is shown using this tag N5 and for Higher students, this tag: H

After this introduction, there are two extracts, both of which you will need to refer to at several points throughout the book.

All question types which you will encounter in the exam are covered in this book. For these question types, we have provided an example passage, question and annotated answer, followed by a quick test to check you have understood.

Exam practice is given with full exam-style questions and sample answers.

Passage 1

How to build a time machine

In the following article from the *MailOnline* website Stephen Hawking asks whether time travel is ever likely to take place.

Hello. My name is Stephen Hawking. Physicist, cosmologist and something of a dreamer. Although I cannot move and I have to speak through a computer, in my mind I am free. Free to explore the universe and ask the big questions, such as: is time travel possible? Can we open a
5 portal to the past or find a shortcut to the future? Can we ultimately use the laws of nature to become masters of time itself?

To see how this might be possible, we need to look at time as physicists do – at the fourth dimension. It's not as hard as it sounds. Every attentive schoolchild knows that all physical objects, even me in my chair, exist in
10 three dimensions. Everything has a width and a height and a length.

But there is another kind of length, a length in time. While a human may survive for 80 years, the stones at Stonehenge, for instance, have stood around for thousands of years. And the solar system will last for billions of years. Everything has a length in time as well as space. Travelling in
15 time means travelling through this fourth dimension. But how do we find a path through the fourth dimension?

Let's indulge in a little science fiction for a moment. Time travel movies often feature a vast, energy-hungry machine. The machine creates a path through the fourth dimension, a tunnel through time. A time traveller, a
20 brave, perhaps foolhardy individual, prepared for who knows what, steps into the time tunnel and emerges who knows when. The concept may be far-fetched, and the reality may be very different from this, but the idea itself is not so crazy.

Physicists have been thinking about tunnels in time too, but we come at
25 it from a different angle. We wonder if portals to the past or the future could ever be possible within the laws of nature. As it turns out, we think they are. What's more, we've even given them a name: wormholes. The truth is that wormholes are all around us, only they're too small to see. Wormholes are very tiny. They occur in nooks and crannies in space and
30 time. You might find it a tough concept, but stay with me.

A wormhole is a theoretical 'tunnel' or shortcut, predicted by Einstein's theory of relativity, that links two places in space-time; it is where negative energy pulls space and time into the mouth of a tunnel, emerging in another universe. After all, nothing is flat or solid. If you
35 look closely enough at anything you'll find holes and wrinkles in it. It's

a basic physical principle, and it even applies to time. Something as smooth as a pool ball has tiny crevices, wrinkles and voids. Now it's easy to show that this is true in the first three dimensions. But trust me, it's also true of the fourth dimension. There are tiny crevices, wrinkles
40 and voids in time. Down at the smallest of scales, smaller even than molecules, smaller than atoms, we get to a place called the quantum foam. This is where wormholes exist. Tiny tunnels or shortcuts through space and time constantly form, disappear, and reform within this quantum world. And they actually link two separate places and two
45 different times.

Unfortunately, these real-life time tunnels are just a billion-trillion-trillionths of a centimetre across, much too small for a human to pass through, but some scientists think it may be possible to capture a wormhole and enlarge it many trillions of times to make it big enough
50 for a human or even a spaceship to enter.

Given enough power and advanced technology, perhaps a giant wormhole could even be constructed in space. I'm not saying that this can be done, but if it could be, it would be a truly remarkable device. One end could be here near Earth, and the other far, far away, near
55 some distant planet.

Theoretically, a time tunnel or wormhole could do even more than take us to other planets. If both ends were in the same place, and separated by time instead of distance, a ship could fly in and come out still near Earth, but in the distant past. Maybe dinosaurs would witness the ship
60 coming in for a landing.

But then we come up against the problem of paradoxes: paradoxes are fun to think about. The most famous one is usually called the Grandfather paradox, but my new, simpler version is called the Mad Scientist paradox. This chap is determined to create a paradox, even
65 if it costs him his life. Imagine, somehow, he's built a wormhole, a time tunnel that stretches just one minute into the past. Through the wormhole, the scientist can see himself as he was one minute ago. But

what if our scientist uses the wormhole to shoot his earlier self? He's now dead. So who fired the shot? It's a paradox. It just doesn't make
70 sense. It's the sort of situation that gives cosmologists nightmares.

This kind of time machine would violate a fundamental rule that governs the entire universe – that causes happen before effects, and never the other way around. I believe things can't make themselves impossible. If they could then there'd be nothing to stop the whole universe from
75 descending into chaos. So I think something will always happen that prevents the paradox. Somehow there must be a reason why our scientist will never find himself in a situation where he could shoot himself. And in this case, I'm sorry to say, the wormhole itself is the problem.

In the end, I think a wormhole like this one can't exist. And the reason
80 for that is feedback. As soon as the wormhole expands, natural radiation will enter it, and end up in a loop. The feedback will become so strong it destroys the wormhole. So although tiny wormholes do exist, and it may be possible to inflate one some day, it won't last long enough to be of use as a time machine.

85 Any kind of time travel to the past through wormholes or any other method is probably impossible, otherwise paradoxes would occur. So sadly, it looks like time travel to the past is never going to happen. A disappointment for dinosaur hunters and a relief for historians.

Passage 2

The big question

Steve Connor, Science Editor of *The Independent*, asks The Big Question: Is time travel possible, and is there any chance that it will ever take place?

Two Russian mathematicians have suggested that the giant atom-smasher being built at the European centre for nuclear research, Cern, near Geneva, could create the conditionswhere it might be possible to travel backwards or forwards in time. In essence, IrinaAref'eva and Igor Volovich believe that
5 the Large Hadron Collider at Cern might create tiny'wormholes' in space which could allow some form of limited time travel.

It has to be said, however, that few scientists accept the idea that the Large Hadron Collider (LHC) will create the conditions thought to be necessary for time travel. The LHC is designed to probe the mysterious
10 forces that exist at the level of sub-atomic particles, and as such will answer many important questions, such as the true nature of gravity. It is not designed as a time machine.

In any case, if the LHC became a time machine by accident, the device would exist only at the sub-atomic level so we are not talking about a
15 machine like Dr Who's Tardis, which is able to carry people forwards and backwards from the future.

The theoretical possibility is widely debated, but everyone agrees that the practical problems are so immense that it is, in all likelihood, never going to happen. Brian Cox, a Cern researcher at the University of Manchester,
20 points out that even if the laws of physics do not prohibit time travel, that doesn't mean to say it's going to happen, certainly in terms of travelling back in time.

'Time travel into the future is absolutely possible; in fact time passes at a different rate in orbit than it does on the ground, and this has to be taken
25 into consideration in order for satellite navigation systems to work. But time travel into the past, although technically allowed in Einstein's theory, will in the opinion of most physicists be ruled out when, and if, we develop a better understanding of the fundamental laws of physics – and that's what the LHC is all about.'

30　It comes down to the general theory of relativity devised by Albert Einstein in 1915. It is the best theory we have so far on the nature of space and time and it was Einstein who first formulated the mathematical equations that related both time and space in the form of an entity called 'space-time'. Those equations and the theory itself do not
35　prohibit the idea of time travel, although there have been many attempts since Einstein to prove that travelling back in time is impossible.

Lots of science fiction writers have had fun with time travel, going back to H.G. Wells, whose book *The Time Machine* was published in 1895 – 20 years before Einstein's general theory of relativity. Interestingly, it was another
40　attempt at science fiction that revived the modern interest in time travel.

When Carl Sagan, the American astronomer, was writing his 1985 novel *Contact*, he wanted a semi-plausible way of getting round the problem of not being able to travel faster than the speed of light – which would break a fundamental rule of physics. He needed his characters to travel through vast
45　distances in space, so he asked his cosmologist friend Kip Thorne to come up with a possible way of doing it without travelling faster than light.

Thorne suggested that by manipulating black holes it might be possible to create a 'wormhole' through space-time that would allow someone to travel from one part of the Universe to another in an instant. He later
50　realised that this could also in theory be used to travel back in time. It was just a theory of course, and no one has come close to solving the practical problem of manipulating black holes and creating wormholes, but the idea seemed to be sound. It spawned a lot of subsequent interest in wormholes and time travel, hence the latest idea by the two Russian
55　mathematicians.

The biggest theoretical problem is known as the time-travel paradox. If someone travels back in time and does something to prevent their own existence, then how can time travel be possible? The classic example is the time traveller who kills his grandfather before his own father is
60　conceived.

The science writer and physicist John Gribbin, who explains these things better than most, has said: 'The snag is that the kind of accidental "time tunnel" that could be produced by the LHC in Geneva would be a tiny wormhole far smaller than an atom, so nothing would be able to go
65　through it. So there won't be any visitors from the future turning up in Geneva just yet. I'd take it all with a pinch of salt, but it certainly isn't completely crazy.'

So, not completely crazy, just a bit crazy.

Question types

There are four question types at N5 and five question types at Higher in the Reading for Understanding, Analysis and Evaluation papers.

Type 1 questions – understanding

Type 1 questions require you to demonstrate your understanding of some aspect of the passage by using your own words. Questions can be in three forms:

- asking you to explain an idea conveyed by the writer
- asking you to identify an aspect of the passage
- asking you to demonstrate how a sentence links the writer's ideas and arguments

If the question asks you to explain an idea, then you will have to express the writer's ideas or point of view in your own words.

If the question asks you to identify an aspect of the passage, you will be referred to a specific part of the passage.

If the question asks you to show how a sentence or paragraph links the writer's arguments or ideas, then quote the words that link back, demonstrate the link back to the idea contained in the previous paragraphs, quote the words that link forward to the development of the writer's argument, then demonstrate the link forward to that idea or argument.

Always use your own words. You can use bullet points if that helps.

Type 2 questions – language

Type 2 questions require analysis of language, including:

- word choice
- sentence structure
- imagery
- tone

In your answers to Type 2 questions, you must quote directly from the given passage then give a detailed analysis of your chosen quotation. You may be asked to evaluate an image. In these questions, you will be expected to say whether or not you find the image appropriate.

With Type 2 questions, there is an important difference between N5 and Higher: in N5 you are awarded a mark for the selected quotation, but there are no marks for your chosen quotation at Higher.

H The Higher Reading for Understanding, Analysis and Evaluation paper has more language questions than is the case at N5.

Type 3 questions – effectiveness

Type 3 questions require you to explain the effectiveness of a particular aspect of a piece of writing. Questions can be in two forms:

- explain the effectiveness of an opening paragraph
- explain the effectiveness of a conclusion

In questions about the effectiveness of an opening paragraph, look for: an opening sentence that grabs the reader's attention, an indication of the subject matter of the passage, unusual sentence structure, use of alliteration or other language techniques.

In questions about the effectiveness of a conclusion, look for and refer to a point made (a word or phrase or expression) in the conclusion and then find a reference to a similar point (or the same point) earlier in the extract.

Sometimes you will find an illustrative example in the conclusion. Show how it illustrates the argument being made in the extract.

Type 4 questions – summarise

In Type 4 questions, you will be asked to summarise a specific part of the passage or of the writer's argument. Look for the main points and use bullet points to put them into your own words. Do not give details, such as examples, but try to generalise.

Type 5 questions – comparing passages

H Type 5 questions ask you to identify a number of key areas from the two passages where the writers either agree or disagree. You will be given a brief statement of the theme of both passages.

You should support the points you make by referring to appropriate, important ideas.

Use these steps for all your questions and answers.

- Read the question carefully and note what you are being asked to do.
- Underline the relevant areas of text.
- Always use your own words, giving an explanation relevant to the question.
- You can write in continuous prose or bullet points.
- The number of marks in the question will be a guide to the number of points you should make.

Understanding

Explaining an idea

Questions that ask you to explain an idea frequently occur in the N5 Reading for Understanding, Analysis and Evaluation paper. To answer these questions correctly, you must deal with the writer's ideas, but you must use your own words.

The wording of these questions is usually straightforward, asking you to explain an aspect of the writer's ideas. The question could be framed as:

In what way(s)

or

Explain

Read the following extract taken from an article by Tom Bolton about the history of London's rivers.

London once needed all the rivers it could get: for drinking water, for harbours and wharves, for mills, for tanneries, and for sluicing away waste. The rivers were London's sewage system long before any system was conceived, but even tiny medieval London was too much for any stream to cope with. The Walbrook, flowing through the heart of the City of London, was mostly paved over in the 1460s; it was considered a filthy nuisance choked with refuse. London's origins are deep in the Walbrook, the river around which the Romans founded the city. The debris dug from the river – hoes and ploughshares, chisels and saws, scalpels and spatulas, the heads of forgotten gods and a collection of 48 human skulls tell the earliest London tales.

As London began to grow at the end of the 18th century, and then to mushroom beyond reason during the 19th century, the rivers became a big problem. Floods, filth, stench and disease put off Georgian and Victorian house-buyers. In Mayfair, the Tyburn was tucked away under mews. In West Norwood, the Effra was buried deep under grids of new Victorian villas.

1 Read the first two sentences of the extract and explain briefly why, according to the writer, London needed its rivers. [2]

The relevant parts of the text have been underlined for you. There are two marks for the question, therefore you need to make two points.

The first sentence lists London's need for rivers: for drinking water, for harbours and wharves, for mills, for tanneries, and for sluicing away waste – six reasons in all, if you count harbours and wharves as two reasons.

The second sentence makes clear that the rivers were needed to help remove sewage from London.

The writer claims that London needed its rivers because they provided harbour facilities **[1]** and they also supplied power for mills **[1]**.

2 Read the second paragraph. Explain why, according to the writer, London's rivers became a big problem. **[2]**

Again, the relevant parts of the text have been underlined for you. You need to make two points to earn two marks.

The writer explains that London's rivers became a big problem as London grew enormously during the 19th century **[1]** and the rivers began to cause disgusting smells and ill health **[1]**.

> ## Questions

QUICK TEST
Read the passage opposite for Questions 1 and 2.
1. Read the last sentence of the first paragraph. Explain what, according to the writer, the debris, dug from the river Walbrook, reveals about early London.
2. Read the last two sentences of the second paragraph and explain what solution was found for the unpleasant rivers.

Identifying facts or ideas

Questions that ask you to identify facts or ideas are not common in N5 Reading for Understanding, Analysis and Evaluation, but they do occur from time to time.

Read this passage for Question 1. The passage is taken from an article by Matthew Syed about flight-fight-freeze responses to alarming situations.

If you throw a rat into the middle of a room full of humans, <u>it will instinctively freeze</u>. By becoming <u>completely still</u>, it is more likely to <u>avoid detection</u>. Then, <u>it will dart into a corner of the room, hoping to flee danger. If cornered, however, it will fight</u>. Ferociously.

Psychologists call it the fight-flight-freeze response, and it emerged very early in evolution. We know this because it is common to all vertebrates. The response starts in the amygdala, an almond-shaped part of the brain, which lights up like a Christmas tree when an animal is confronted by a threat and is controlled by the automatic nervous system. This is the same system that manages digestion and respiration, and is independent of conscious will.

1 Identify three things a rat will do if it is thrown into a room full of humans. **[3]**

The relevant parts of the text have been underlined. If you read them carefully, they indicate all the reactions of rat behaviour under such circumstances.

There are 3 marks for the question, so you must make three points in your answer.

The rat will go very still (freeze) **[1]**. It will retreat to ensure no one sees it (flee) **[1]**. It will confront its opponents violently (fight) **[1]**.

You need only choose two of the above for 2 marks.

Read this passage for Question 2. The passage is taken from an article on attitudes to immigration by Ruth Wishart.

The city census of 1831 found 47 Jewish citizens, a community which <u>grew and prospered</u> as it became an <u>integral part of Glasgow's merchant growth</u>. The first Asian immigrants were no more than a few dozen young men, largely from poor rural backgrounds, whose early employment as door-to-door salesmen gave no hint of the <u>entrepreneurial flair their heirs and successors would bring to so many trade sectors in the city</u>.

The <u>early Italians found the route to Glaswegian hearts through their stomachs as they set up chains of chip shops and ice-cream parlours</u>; and the <u>Chinese, too, helped the local palate</u> become rather more discerning when they began to arrive in numbers half a century ago.

2 Identify two similarities between Asian and Jewish immigrants to Glasgow and identify one similarity between Chinese and Italian immigrants to Glasgow. **[3]**

The relevant points have been underlined. To complete your answer, identify those parts you have underlined and rewrite using your own words.

Read the question carefully. There are 2 marks for identifying similarities between Asian and Jewish immigrants, so you must make 2 points about Asian and Jewish immigrants.

Asian and Jewish immigrants were financially successful. Both groups benefited Glasgow's economy over time **[2]**. Italians and Chinese developed food outlets in Glasgow **[1]**.

> **Questions**

QUICK TEST
Read the passage about immigration in Glasgow for Questions 1–3.
1. Identify the effect on Glasgow of the Jewish citizens discovered by the 1831 city census.
2. Identify the effect on Glasgow of the Chinese when they arrived 50 years ago.
3. Identify two points that the writer makes about the 'first Asian immigrants'.

Understanding

Linking ideas

In questions that ask you to make links, you have to demonstrate how a given sentence links the writer's ideas or arguments.

Sometimes questions ask you to explain the function of a sentence in the development of the writer's argument.

Always read the question carefully. Is it about the writer's argument or about ideas?

Links between ideas can be formed using conjunctions such as *and, but,* and *or.* Look out for questions which the writer goes on to answer: the question may well link back, and the answer may well be the link forward.

Read this passage for Question 1. In this passage, the design and architecture writer Deyan Sudjic is discussing the growth of cities.

The future of the city has suddenly become the only subject in town. It ranges from tough topics such as managing water resources, economic policy, transport planning, racial tolerance and law enforcement to what is usually presented as the fluffier end of the scale, such as making public spaces people want to spend time in and deciding the colour of the buses. But it is this diversity which powerfully affirms the city as mankind's greatest single invention.

<u>For all their agonies</u>, cities must be counted as a <u>positive force</u>. They are an <u>engine of growth</u>, a machine for putting the rural poor onto the first rung of <u>urban prosperity and freedom</u>. Look at London, a city that existed for several centuries before anything approximating England had been thought of. It has a far stronger sense of itself and its identity than Britain as a whole or England. It has grown, layer on layer, for 2000 years, sustaining generation after generation of newcomers.

1 Explain the function of the first two lines of the second paragraph – 'For all their agonies … urban prosperity and freedom' – in the development of the writer's argument. **[2]**

The relevant references have been underlined for you. The phrase 'For all their agonies' links back to the problems to do with the management and policing of cities discussed in the first paragraph. The phrase 'positive force' links forward to the ideas presented later in the second paragraph that a city such as London has supported influxes of individuals and their families to the city over thousands of years.

Answers could include:

The phrase 'For all their agonies' links back to the problems of managing and policing cities [1], while the phrase 'positive force' links forward to the idea that a city such as London has supported incomers to the city over thousands of years [1].

The phrase 'urban prosperity and freedom' in the second paragraph links back to the idea presented at the end of the first paragraph that cities have been our greatest invention [1], while the phrase 'engine of growth' points forward to the idea of the city's continuing ability to support so many people over such a long time [1].

Questions

QUICK TEST

Read carefully Passage 1, *How to build a time machine* by Stephen Hawking, about time travel on pages 5–7.

1. Explain how the sentence in line 11 (paragraph 3, begins 'But there is another kind of length') provides a link between the writer's ideas at this point.

2. Explain how the sentence in lines 71–73 (paragraph 11, beginning 'This kind of time machine ...') provides a link in the writer's argument at this point.

*The words 'this', 'that, 'these' and 'those' are **demonstrative adjectives**: each refers to something mentioned previously and therefore indicates a link.*

Language

Word choice

Questions concerning word choice are language questions. Usually, the question asks you to show how the writer uses language to express an opinion or emphasise support for a point.

When you answer questions involving word choice, make sure you choose the easiest examples to analyse. If you do not know, or are not sure, what a word means, it's best to leave it alone.

In your answer, use the formula 'reference + comment' based on the connotations selected.

In N5, you are given 1 mark for each appropriate quotation and 1 mark for analysis of that reference.

In Higher, there are no marks for quotation, but you must quote. Marks are for the quality of your analysis. For a 4-mark question, you can give two quotations + developed comments OR four quotations with more basic comments.

Read this passage for Question 1. In this passage, the journalist Matthew Syed is writing about the importance of playing football when he was growing up.

My best friend, Mark, was a keen footballer. We played in my back garden <u>every afternoon as kids</u>, often down the local park, <u>sometimes other kids would join us</u>, and <u>in the summer we never seemed to leave</u>.

I often think of those long, <u>endlessly absorbing</u> days, <u>game after game</u>, <u>sometimes until it got dark</u> and we played by the <u>dim glow of street lights</u>. In the summer holidays, my mum would make a two-litre bottle of orange squash and we would <u>pass it from player to player</u> at half-time, <u>none of us deterred by</u> the fact it had got warm in the sun. My, it tasted good.

1 Explain how one example of the writer's word choice makes it clear that his memories of childhood football are positive. **[2]**

The relevant words have been underlined for you. Use the formula 'reference + comment'. You could choose any of these pairs below to gain the 2 marks.

N5 *Answers could include:*

'every afternoon' **[1]** *suggests that football was their major pastime* **[1]**

'sometimes other kids would join us' **[1]** *the sport was so popular that friends helped expand the game* **[1]**

'sometimes until it got dark' **[1]** *[or 'dim glow of street lights'* **[1]***] suggests that they played well after dusk, they so enjoyed it* **[1]**

H 'every afternoon' suggests that not only was football their major pastime **[1]**, but it was a daily occurrence **[1]**

Read this passage for Question 2. In this passage, the writer Jef Costello is writing about what James Bond means in contemporary society.

James Bond is a modern hero, a hero for the modern age. Actually, this claim has often been made. But I mean it in a special sense: Bond is a hero *in spite of* modernity; an anti-modern hero who manages to triumph over – and, indeed, harness – the very forces that turn most modern men into soulless, gelded appendages to their desktop PCs. In this modern world we are all functionaries and office flunkies. *This* is why Bond is important, and this is why we've worshipped at the cinematic altar of Bond for half a century. We long to be as free as he is.

2 By referring to word choice, analyse how the writer emphasises the inferiority of 'most modern men'. **[2]**

N5 Answers could include:

'soulless, gelded appendages' **[1]** suggests that most modern men are fairly drab, characterless people **[1]**

'desktop PCs' **[1]** suggests that they are deskbound, with nothing more exciting to do than work a computer; they are hidebound by computer-orientated tasks **[1]**

'we are all functionaries' **[1]** suggests that modern man is nothing more than a serving bureaucrat **[1]**

H 'soulless, gelded appendages' suggests men who are merely stuck/attached to their computers and have consequently lost their manhood **[2]**

> ## Questions
>
> QUICK TEST
> Read the passage above about James Bond to answer Questions 1 and 2.
> 1. Explain how the writer uses word choice to convey how Bond is an 'anti-modern hero'.
> 2. By referring to word choice, analyse why, in the writer's opinion, 'Bond is important'.

Language

Sentence structure

Sentence structure techniques include lists, climax, repetition, long and short sentences, inversion, unusual word order and changes in tense.

- Lists – often contain climax; suggest range, variety and extent of point being illustrated; use of **tricolon** (a series of three parallel words, phrases or clauses).

- **Climax** – sentences may be structured so that the main point comes at the end, creating climax.

- **Repetition** – intensifies the point being made; creates a climactic build-up to an important final point; intensifies meaning through cumulative or **incremental intensification**; watch out for the repetition of phrases or clauses (known also as **anaphora**) at the beginning of or within a sentence.

- Long sentence followed by a short one – where the dramatic impact falls on the **short sentence**.

- **Inversion** – where the normal order of a sentence is reversed, such that the main point is delayed to the end for emphasis.

- Unusual word order – an **adverb** or a **prepositional phrase** placed at the beginning of a sentence, or at the beginning of a series of sentences, drawing attention to the first word in each case.

- Sudden change in **tense** – often from the past to the present but sometimes from the future to the present. The sudden use of the present tense intensifies the immediacy of the situation. The sudden use of present tense can help indicate the drama of a situation.

Lists 1

Read this passage for Question 1. This is taken from an article by the journalist Isabel Oakeshott about intensive farming in Central Valley, California.

On a cold, bright November day I stood among a million almond trees and breathed in the sweet air. I was in Central Valley, California, in an orchard stretching over 700,000 acres. Before me was a vision of how the British countryside may look one day. <u>Beyond the almond orchards were fields of pomegranates, pistachios, grapes and apricots.</u> Somewhere in the distance were almost two million dairy cows, producing six billion dollars' worth of milk a year.

It may sound like the Garden of Eden but it is a deeply disturbing place. <u>Among the perfectly aligned rows of trees and cultivated crops are no birds, no butterflies, no beetles or shrubs.</u> There is not a single blade of grass or a hedgerow, and the only bees arrive by lorry, transported across the United States. The bees are hired by the day to fertilise the blossom, part of a multibillion-dollar industry that has sprung up to do a job that nature once did for free.

As for the cows, they last only two or three years, ten to fifteen years less than their natural life span. <u>Crammed into barren pens on tiny patches of land, they stand around listlessly waiting to be fed, milked or injected with antibiotics.</u> Through a combination of selective breeding, artificial diets and growth hormones designed to maximise milk production, they are pushed so grotesquely beyond their natural limit that they are soon worn out. In their short lives they never see grass.

1 By referring to sentence structure, analyse how the writer conveys a positive aspect of the Central Valley. [2]

The relevant sentences have been underlined for you. The list of 'pomegranates, pistachios, grapes and apricots' demonstrates the range of crops grown in the area. The list illustrates the variety and exotic nature of the different crops.

N5 *The list [1] in the fourth sentence of the first paragraph illustrates the abundance of fruit and trees grown in the Central Valley [1].*

H *The list in the fourth sentence of the first paragraph exemplifies the abundance of fruit and trees grown in the Central Valley [1] as well as the variety and exotic nature of the different crops [1].*

Questions

QUICK TEST

Read the passage opposite about farming in California to answer Questions 1–3.

1. With reference to the first sentence, show how the writer uses sentence structure to describe the pleasantness of the Central Valley.
2. With reference to sentence structure, show how the last sentence of the first paragraph ('Somewhere in the distance … a year') conveys the productiveness of the Valley.
3. With reference to sentence structure, show how in the last sentence of the passage ('In their short lives they never see grass') the writer conveys disapproval of the treatment of the cows.

Language

Lists 2

Read the passage on pages 20–21 about farming in California for Questions 1 and 2.

1 By referring to one example of sentence structure, analyse how the writer creates a negative impression of Central Valley. **[2]**

The underlined sentence includes the list 'no birds, no butterflies, no beetles or shrubs'. To gain the 2 marks, your answer must include the recognition of the list and its effect.

N5 *Answers could include:*

The list in the second sentence of the second paragraph [1] illustrates and highlights the complete lack of wildlife and plants [1].

H *The list in the second sentence of the second paragraph illustrates the range and extent of the items [1] that highlight the complete lack of wildlife and plants [1].*

The repetition of the 'no' [1] in the list in the second sentence of the second paragraph illustrates the complete lack of wildlife and plants [1] in the Central Valley.

2 By referring to sentence structure, analyse how the writer makes clear her disapproval of dairy farming methods used in Central Valley. **[2]**

The list relating to dairy farming has three items in it and is a tricolon. By placing the item 'injected with antibiotics' at the end of the list, the writer draws attention to the process of administering healthy animals with a drug for the wrong reasons.

N5 *Answers could include:*

Each item in the tricolon – 'fed', 'milked', 'injected with antibiotics' [1] – increases in length, building to a climax [1].

The climax [1] highlights the unnecessary use of medicine at the end of a production-line process [1].

H *The tricolon 'they stand around listlessly waiting to be fed, milked or injected with antibiotics', where each item – 'fed', 'milked', 'injected with antibiotics' – increases in length, builds up to and highlights [1] the climactic point concerning the unnecessary use of medicine at the end of a production-line process [1].*

Read this sentence for Question 3, taken from an article by Rob Edwards about the Scottish government's plans to cut pollution.

Stricter and lower speed limits, higher parking charges and a five pence per kilometre road pricing scheme are being proposed by the Scottish government as part of a major new offensive to cut the pollution that is disrupting the climate.

3 By referring to sentence structure, analyse how the writer conveys the significance of the government's schemes. **[2]**

N5 *The use of the list [1] at the beginning of the sentence draws attention to and highlights the importance of the variety and extent of the measures that the Scottish government want to introduce to deal with pollution [1].*

H *The use of the tricolon, placed at the beginning of the sentence, draws attention to and thereby highlights the importance of the variety and extent of the measures that the government want to put in place to alleviate pollution [2]. The tricolon itself highlights the climactic point ('a five pence per kilometre road pricing scheme'), thereby signifying it as the most important measure they want to put in place [2].*

Questions

QUICK TEST
Read this passage for Questions 1 and 2, taken from an article by Ian Wooldridge about the boxer Muhammad Ali.

In 1960, in racist, reactionary, bigoted small-town America, uppity young black men were lucky enough to get one break, let alone two.

Destiny determined otherwise. A legend was in the making. What overwhelms you about this man from such a violent trade are the goodness, sincerity and generosity that have survived a lifetime of controversy, racial hatred, fundamental religious conversion, criminal financial exploitation, marital upheavals, revilement by many of his own nation, and, eventually, the collapse of his own body.

N5 1. Show how the writer uses sentence structure to convey his disapproval of 'small-town America'.

H 2. Show how the writer uses sentence structure to convey how impressed he was about Muhammad Ali's personality.

Inversion and climax

Inversion and climax are used to draw attention to particular important ideas. In questions about inversion and climax, you must be able to identify the technique and analyse the effect.

Read this passage for Question 1. The passage is the opening paragraph of an article by Carol Midgley on the attraction of shopping.

> This is a story about modern consumerism; it is being written inside a mall. From my vantage point on a wooden bench purposely designed to be uncomfortable and placed alongside a digital screen pulsing ever-changing adverts selling other outlets, other products, other ways here to spend, spend, spend, <u>I can watch shoals of people hurrying in and out of stores honouring the creed of the turbo-consumer: live to shop</u>.

1 Show how the writer's use of language emphasises the intensity of consumerism. **[2]**

The second sentence uses inversion, placing the main point 'I can watch shoals of people hurrying in and out of stores honouring the creed of turbo-consumerism: live to shop' at the end of the sentence.

N5 *The use of the colon [1] at the end of the paragraph signals the whole point of the sentence – the importance of shopping [1].*

H *The use of inversion in the second sentence delays the climax, creating a build-up to the expression 'live to shop' [1] and conveying the intensity of consumerism by highlighting that the whole point of living is to buy goods [1].*

Read this passage for Question 2. This is taken from an article arguing that young people's mental abilities can come from popular culture and video games in particular.

> Where most critics allege a dumbing down, <u>I see a progressive story</u>: popular culture steadily, but almost imperceptibly, making our brains sharper as we soak in entertainment usually dismissed as so much lowbrow fluff. I hope to persuade you that increasingly the non-literary popular culture is honing different mental skills that are just as important as the ones exercised by reading books.

2 By referring to sentence structure, show how the writer demonstrates his approval of popular culture and video games. **[2]**

N5 The writer highlights 'I see a progressive story' by placing it at the end of the sentence before the colon **[1]**, indicating how positively he regards popular culture **[1]**.

H By using inversion before the colon, the writer highlights 'I see a progressive story' **[1]**, drawing attention to his modern encouraging view of popular culture **[1]**.

Questions

QUICK TEST

N5 1. Read this passage, taken from an article by Jason Diamond on the Literary Hub website.

When I walk into Community Bookstore in Brooklyn, my local, the first thing I do (after saying hi to the owners) is look for the store cat, Tiny the Usurper.

By referring to sentence structure, show how the writer creates an element of the unexpected in this opening sentence.

H 2. Read this sentence from an article by Melanie Reid. She alleges that the success of JK Rowling's *Harry Potter* books has to do with clever marketing.

Where I really quarrel with *Harry Potter* is not in the quality of the writing but in the marketing.

By referring to sentence structure of the above sentence, show how the writer makes clear her attitude to the *Harry Potter* books.

Repetition

Repetition is used frequently in prose, drama and especially poetry. Journalists often use repetition to reinforce a point being made. One of the effects of repetition is **cumulative intensification**, where the point made is intensified by the use of repetition.

Read this passage for Question 1. This is taken from an article by Matthew Syed about the ways athletes respond to pressure in their sport.

> This, I think, is what top athletes mean when they repeat that otherwise paradoxical saying: "Pressure is not a problem; it is a privilege". Talk to David Beckham, Sebastian Coe or Sir Chris Hoy and <u>they will be perfectly open</u> about their nerves and fear. But <u>they also talk</u> with great pride about facing up to them. <u>They didn't see</u> these human responses as signs of weakness but as opportunities to grow. <u>They created mechanisms</u> (often highly personal ones) to help them through. <u>They seized every opportunity</u> to face danger and learnt from each experience.

1 Explain what the attitude of top athletes is to pressure, and how two examples of the language used make this attitude clear. **[3]**

N5 *There are five repetitions of 'They + verb'. This highlights the fact that the athletes discuss their attitudes to pressure, but that they also adopt a positive way of dealing with it. There is 1 mark for stating the attitude, and 2 marks for the quality of the comment.*

> Their attitude is very constructive **[1]**. The repetition of 'They + verb' shows that they share a positive attitude towards pressure, shown by the positive connotations of the verbs used **[2]**.

Read this passage for Question 2. The passage is taken from an article by Melanie Reid in which she is complaining that there are too many safety restrictions on children.

> <u>I am</u> fed up listening to scaremongers talking about the E-coli virus, telling me my child should never visit a farm or come into contact with animals. <u>I am</u> very weary of organisations that are dedicated to promulgating the idea that threats and dangers to children lurk everywhere. <u>I am</u> sick of charities who on the one hand attack overprotective parents and at the same time say children should never be left unsupervised in public places.

Everywhere you turn there is an army of professionals – ably abetted by the media – hard at work encouraging parents to fear the worst. Don't let your children out in the sun – not unless they are wearing special UV-resistant T-shirts. Don't buy your child a Wendyhouse, they might crush their fingers on the hinges. Don't buy a baby walker, your toddlers might brain themselves. Don't buy plastic baby teethers, your baby might suck in harmful chemicals. Don't let them use mobile phones, they'll sizzle their brains. Don't buy a second-hand car seat, it will not protect them. And on and on it goes.

2 By referring to sentence structure in the first paragraph, explain how Melanie Reid shows her disapproval of those who are overprotective of children. **[2]**

H *She repeats 'I am' at the beginning of three sentences:*

- *I am fed up listening …*
- *I am weary of …*
- *I am sick of …*

This builds up from the fairly mild tone in the first sentence 'I am fed up' to the more intense tone in the final sentence 'I am sick …'. She uses repetition to increase her intensification of the point being made.

H *The writer's use of repetition at the beginning of three sentences (anaphora) slowly builds up* **[1]** *her feelings of disapproval from a mild tone ('I am fed up') to an angry tone ('I am sick')* **[1]**.

> ## Questions
>
> QUICK TEST
> Read the first passage on page 26 for Questions 1 and 2.
> 1. Explain how one example of word choice conveys the writer's attitude to the athletes.
> 2. Explain how one example of word choice reveals that nothing could spoil their enjoyment.
> Read the second passage on page 26 for Question 3.
> 3. By referring to sentence structure, explain how the writer shows her feelings of frustration at so many health and safety demands.

Words and phrases at the beginning of a sentence

A writer might invert (or **transpose**) the position of a word or phrase by placing it at the beginning of a sentence in order to highlight the point being made.

Read this passage for Question 1. The passage is from the book *Impact! The Threat of Comets and Asteroids* by Gerrit Verschuur. The author outlines the sequence of events that took place over billions of years.

A lot has been learned about the nature of cosmic collisions and this new knowledge has given a remarkable twist to the story of our origins. We now recognise that comet and asteroid impacts may be the most important driving force behind evolutionary change on the planet. <u>Originally</u>, such objects smashed into one another to build the Earth 4·5 billion years ago. <u>After that</u>, further comet impacts brought the water of our oceans and the organic molecules needed for life. <u>Ever since then</u>, impacts have continued to punctuate the story of evolution. <u>On many occasions</u>, comets slammed into Earth with such violence that they nearly precipitated the extinction of all life. <u>In the aftermath</u> of each catastrophe, new species emerged to take the place of those that had been wiped out.

1 Analyse how the writer uses language to develop his idea that comet and asteroid impacts helped the formation of the Earth. **[4]**

The writer's point is that evolutionary change has been driven by asteroid impacts over the lifetime of the Earth. The sentences from 'Originally, such objects … wiped out' develop that idea by placing a word or phrases relating to time – 'Originally', 'After that', 'Ever since then', 'On many occasions', 'In the aftermath' (all adverbs of time) – at the beginning of each, setting out the chronological sequence of events from the formation of the Earth to the emergence of new life-forms.

By using time-related words **[1]** – 'Originally', 'After that', 'Ever since then', 'On many occasions', 'In the aftermath' – at the beginning of the five sentences **[1]**, the writer clarifies the chronology of change that took place from the formation of our planet **[1]** to the emergence, after several impacts, of new life-forms **[1]**.

Read this passage for Question 2, taken from the essay *Marrakech* by George Orwell. He is reflecting on the primitive conditions in which the carpenter works his lathe.

A carpenter sits cross-legged at a prehistoric lathe, turning chair-legs at lightning speed. He works the lathe with a bow in his right hand and guides the chisel with his left foot, and thanks to a lifetime of sitting in this position his left leg is warped out of shape. <u>At his side</u>, <u>his grandson</u>, <u>aged six</u>, is already starting on the simpler parts of the job.

2 With reference to sentence structure, show how Orwell conveys his concern for the lack of change in working conditions in Marrakech. **[4]**

The inverted words and phrases have been underlined for you. The main part of the final sentence is kept to the end.

N5 *The phrases 'At his side', 'his grandson' and 'aged six'* **[1]** *have been placed at the beginning of the sentence* **[1]**, *and by delaying the main point 'starting on the simpler parts of the job' to the end* **[1]**, *highlight the idea that the grandson will end up like his grandfather* **[1]**.

H *Orwell shows his concern for the carpenter's grandson by piling up the phrases 'At his side', 'his grandson' and 'aged six' at the beginning of the sentence* **[2]**, *delaying the main point to the end – that the very young grandson will also spend his entire life doing this job and will end up crippled like his grandfather* **[2]**.

Questions

QUICK TEST
Read lines 40–42 of Passage 1 on page 6 (paragraph 6, the sentence beginning 'Down at the smallest of scales …').
By referring to sentence structure, show how Hawking conveys his attitude to quantum foam.

Language

Long sentence followed by a short one

In order to draw attention to a point being made, writers will often follow a long sentence with a short dramatic one.

Read this passage for Question 1. In this passage, Gerald Early describes his success with a baseball bat.

I used that bat the entire summer and a magical season it was. I was the best hitter in the neighbourhood. Once, I won a game in the last at-bat with a home run, and the boys just crowded round me as if I were a spectacle to behold, as if I were, for one small moment, in this insignificant part of the world, playing in this meaningless game, their majestic, golden prince.

<u>But the bat broke</u>. Some kid used it without my permission. He hit a foul ball and the bat split, the barrel flying away, the splintered handle still in the kid's hands.

1 Show how the writer's use of language in the second paragraph conveys the impact of the destruction of the bat. **[2]**

In the first paragraph, the last sentence is long. This is followed by a short four-word sentence at the start of the next paragraph. The short sentence 'But the bat broke' is a dramatic anti-climax. The writer also uses alliteration of the plosive 'b' sound, highlighting the drama, capturing the sound of a breaking bat.

The short sentence at the beginning of the paragraph **[1]** is both dramatic and anti-climactic, drawing attention to the violent end to the bat **[1]**.

Read this passage for Question 2. In this passage, George Orwell describes the time when he shot an elephant in Burma (now Myanmar).

But in falling he seemed for a moment to rise, for as his hind legs collapsed beneath him he seemed to tower upwards like a huge rock toppling, his trunk reaching skywards like a tree. He trumpeted, for the first and only time. And then down he came, his belly towards me, with a crash that seemed to shake the ground even where I lay.

<u>I got up</u>. The Burmans were already racing past me across the mud.

2 Show how the writer's use of language in the second paragraph draws attention to the sudden change that takes place. **[2]**

Note the contrast between the long sentences at the end of the first paragraph and the very short three-word sentence at the beginning of the next paragraph.

As the elephant falls, the narrator gets up, but the shortness of the sentence highlights the drama, signalling the finality of the episode.

The writer's simple quick movement described in the short sentence at the beginning of the second paragraph contrasts **[1]** with the long sentence that has described the slow death of the elephant, drawing attention to the fact that the shooting of the elephant is finally over **[1]**.

> ## Questions
>
> QUICK TEST
> Read this passage by the Scottish writer William McIlvanney.
>
> My mother was a ferocious carer who had an almost mystical capacity to conjure solid worries out of air that to the rest of us looked untroubled and clear. Maybe somebody else was supposed to be with me and had gone out briefly.
>
> I don't know. I am simply aware of myself there. The moment sits separate and vivid in my memory, without explanation, like a rootless flower. Whoever I was being, traveller or knight, I must have been tired. For I feel asleep.
>
> Show how in the second paragraph, the writer reinforces the significance of the moment described in the first paragraph.

Language

Punctuation 1 – Exclamation marks and question marks

Punctuation marks are used by writers to signal meaning. Knowledge of punctuation marks can help in answering questions about sentence structure.

Read this passage for Question 1. This is taken from *How to be a Bad Birdwatcher* by the journalist Simon Barnes.

I was going through Monken Hadley churchyard and there were lots (note scientific precision) of house martins whizzing round the church tower. House martins are dapper little chaps, navy blue with white, and they are one of the sights of the summer: doing things like whizzing round church steeples and catching flies in their beaks. Later in the season the young ones take up whizzing themselves, trying to get the hang of this flying business. So I paused in my journey to spend a few moments gazing at the whirligig of martins. It was nothing special, nothing exceptional, and it was very good indeed. Note this: one of the greatest pleasures in birdwatching is the quiet enjoyment of the absolutely ordinary.

And then it happened. Bam!

Gone!

1 With reference to sentence structure, show how the writer suggests speed in the final two paragraphs of the above extract. **[2]**

Short sentences can be used to convey sudden movement. The second paragraph has only one very short sentence and an interjection (exclamation): 'And then it happened. Bam!'

This raises the reader's expectations, and the ordinariness portrayed by the previous sentences is broken. The exclamation mark after 'Bam!' reinforces the shock created by the 'Bam!'.

The third paragraph is even shorter, with a one-word sentence: 'Gone!'. The reader is left wondering and is compelled to read on to find out what happened next.

The use of the exclamation marks **[1]** after 'Bam!' and 'Gone!' suggest surprise and shock at the speed with which the house martins disappeared **[1]**.

Read this passage for Question 2. This passage is taken from an article by Catherine Bennett about giving 16-year-olds the vote.

There are hugely <u>important questions</u> to address before 16-year-olds can be invited into the complicated UK electoral process. Are they sufficiently mature? Can they tell one party from another? Are they too preoccupied by a combination of exams and hectic social lives to be bothered? Even worrying about their appearance has been cited as a reason why under-18s might struggle to give adequate thought to the political and economic issues facing Britain today.

2 Analyse two ways in which the writer attempts to engage the reader's interest in the opening paragraph. **[2]**

The opening sentence mentions 'important questions', adding significance to the questions that follow. The repeated use of question marks engages the reader's interest by indicating what the questions actually are and inviting the reader to think about them.

The word choice 'important questions' makes clear that the questions are significant and worthy of answers **[1]** and the repeated use of questions helps engage the reader's interest **[1]**.

> ## Questions

QUICK TEST
Read this passage by the journalist Carol Midgley. She is considering the hold shopping has over many people.

How did we get here? How did we get to a point where shopping became the premier leisure activity, where we gladly boarded the work-to-spend treadmill, the insatiable pursuit of "more", which resulted in there being, for example, 121 mobile phones for every 100 people in the UK? Does it even matter? Shopping doesn't kill anyone, it keeps the economy going and provides one in six jobs. If it makes people happy, why not leave them to it?

With reference to language, show how the writer conveys her doubt about the nature of shopping.

Punctuation 2 – Colons and semi-colons

The colon has three main uses:

- to introduce a list

- to signal an explanation or example following a statement

- to introduce a quotation

A single dash is increasingly being used in place of a colon, particularly when introducing a list.

Read this paragraph for Question 1. This is taken from an article by the journalist Janice Turner about the importance of trees.

A posh gardener once suggested we cut down most of our trees and start again with fresh, more groovy varieties. This misunderstood <u>the very point:</u> trees are the antithesis of fickle fashion. But some crass homeowners can't bear the fluff-balls from plane trees messing up their hall carpet of the lime sap puking down on their shiny car bonnets. Neater to reach for the axe. Maybe garden centres should start selling plastic ones: say goodbye to autumnal hell.

1 With reference to the second sentence, show how the writer uses language to convey her irritation. **[2]**

The use of the colon [1] in the first sentence signals an explanation of the 'the very point' – that trees are the opposite of what is regarded as a current trend [1].

The semi-colon has three main uses:

- to indicate a connection between items which in themselves could stand as grammatically independent sentences

- to separate items in a complex list where commas would be insufficient or where commas are already used in items within the list

- to create balance – *To err is human; to forgive divine*

Read this paragraph for Question 2. This is taken from an article by Matthew Syed about the pressures that top sportspeople face in competition.

This, I think, is what top athletes mean when they repeat that otherwise paradoxical saying: "Pressure is not a problem; it is a privilege".

The colon introduces the quotation and the semi-colon signals that the two units of sense 'Pressure is not a problem' and 'it is a privilege' are linked. It also signals that the two units are closely related and it provides balance between them. It helps signal the antithesis (two words that contrast each other) – 'problems' and 'privilege'.

2 Show how the writer uses language to make clear the attitude of athletes towards pressure. **[3]**

15 The colon after 'saying' introduces **[1]** the aphorism (the saying) and the semi-colon after 'problem' **[1]** creates the balance between the two related ideas but emphasises the positive nature of 'privilege' **[1]**.

The colon after 'saying' introduces the aphorism (the saying used by athletes) and the semi-colon after 'problem' creates the balance between the two related but seemingly opposing ideas **[1]**, the binary nature of which alerts the reader to the ideas **[1]** yet emphasises the positive nature of 'privilege' **[1]**.

The marks are awarded for demonstrating how the punctuation helps reveal the athletes' attitudes to pressure.

Questions

QUICK TEST
Read this passage by the journalist Janice Turner about arguments for and against cutting down trees.

Our country's trees will tumble to make way for the machines of progress. But for how much economic growth is it worth mowing down a wood? Trees are beyond priceless: they are our history inscribed in the natural world. Which rich men, planting beautiful orchards to their own glorious memory, have always known.

By closely referring to sentence structure, explain how the writer conveys how much she values trees.

Language

Punctuation 3 – Parenthesis

Parenthesis is used to indicate information which is additional to the sentence but grammatically separate from it. Parenthesis is indicated by paired dashes, paired brackets or paired commas.

The following sentence is taken from an article by Catherine Bennett about the possibility of giving 16-year-olds the vote.

I presumed – without knowing any – that these 16-year-olds were as clueless as my younger self.

The paired dashes signpost 'without knowing any' as parenthetical. This is information that is not part of the grammar of the sentence but is additional to it. In this case it gives the writer's personal experience.

You can remove the parenthesis and the sentence is unaffected grammatically – 'I presumed that these 16-year-olds were as clueless as my younger self'.

Read this passage for Question 1. This is taken from an article by Rachel Johnson about being a parent.

These are the main things, and in these we have, <u>I think we are all agreed</u>, not done too badly. Our children, <u>and I'll generalise here</u>, are not serial axe murderers or kitten drowners. Our children do make an effort <u>– at least on special occasions anyway –</u> to repay the enormous investment of time, energy, money and emotion we have poured into them.

1 Show how the writer's use of language makes clear her positive attitude towards what she regards as 'our children'. **[2]**

The parenthetical phrases are: 'I think we are all agreed', 'and I'll generalise here', 'at least on special occasions anyway'. Each phrase gives the reader added useful information. You can choose any one of them to answer the question.

N5 When the writer says that the children make an effort ' – at least on special occasions anyway –,' her use of parenthesis **[1]** shows that she recognises that they take opportunities of special occasions to repay parents **[1]**.

H The writer's use of the parenthetical ' – at least on special occasions anyway – ' shows that she recognises, even if somewhat grudgingly, that children make special efforts **[1]** to repay the enormity of parental efforts **[1]**.

Read this passage for Question 2. This passage is about Muhammad Ali lighting the torch at the 1996 Olympic Games in Atlanta despite being ill.

It was the best kept secret of the 1996 Olympic Games in Atlanta, at the very heart of America's Deep South, when Ali emerged high in the tower of the stadium to extend a trembling arm and apply, just, a flaming torch to light the Olympic cauldron.

2 Analyse how parenthesis is used to illustrate the 'triumph' and 'tragedy' of Muhammad Ali. **[1]**

The question can be answered by word choice, but also by paying attention to the paired commas.

The parenthetical, ', just,' makes clear that he nearly did not succeed in lighting the torch **[1]**.

Questions

QUICK TEST

Read this paragraph by the journalist Isabel Oakeshott about food production around the world.

But, as I discovered when I began looking into the way food is produced, increasingly powerful forces are pulling us in the opposite direction. We have become addicted to cheap meat, fish and dairy products from supply lines that stretch across the globe. On the plus side, it means that supermarkets can sell whole chickens for as little as £3. Things that were once delicacies, such as smoked salmon, are now as cheap as chips. On the downside, cheap chicken and farmed fish are fatty and flaccid. Industrially reared farm animals – 50 billion of them a year worldwide – are kept permanently indoors, treated like machines and pumped with drugs.

Identify and comment on any examples of parenthesis.

Tense

H Writers occasionally use tense to create special effects, moving from past to present or vice-versa. The effect of using the present tense is usually to create immediacy.

Knowledge about how authors switch tense can be useful at Higher level when analysing sentence structure.

Read this paragraph for Question 1. This is taken from an article by Jay Tate, the director of the Spaceguard Centre in Wales. He is discussing the possible effects of the Earth being hit by a large asteroid.

> In the longer term the problem of being hit by an asteroid <u>will be</u> the amount of material that is injected into the Earth's atmosphere. Within two or three days the surface of <u>the Earth will be cold and dark</u>. And it is the dark which will be the problem, because the plants will begin to die out. At best guess, <u>we will probably lose about 25 per cent of the human population in the first six months or so</u>. The rest of us are basically back in the Middle Ages. <u>We have got no power</u>, no communications, no infrastructure. <u>We are back to the hunter-gathering</u>.

1 Show how Tate's language emphasises the devastating effects of asteroid impact. **[2]**

This question can be answered with reference to tense. The paragraph starts with the future tense: 'the problem ... will be', 'the surface of the Earth will be cold and dark', 'we will probably lose about 25 per cent of the human population in the first six months or so'.

In the next three sentences the tense is switched to the present tense: 'The rest of us are basically back in the Middle Ages. We have got no power, no communications, no infrastructure. We are back to the hunter-gathering.'

The switch from the future tense to the present tense creates an immediacy about the effect of an asteroid impact. The author paints an unpleasant picture of what life will be like for those left alive.

*The use of the present tense reinforces the idea that survival isn't necessarily a benefit for those who live on, as life becomes primitive again. The use of the plural **personal pronoun** also includes the reader, suggesting that they will suffer the consequences of a catastrophic asteroid impact.*

Tate's use of tense helps to emphasise the devastating effects of asteroid impacts. He starts with future tense (suggesting possibility in the future) [1] but then switches to the present tense, creating an immediacy, for the survivors of such a catastrophe [1].

Questions

QUICK TEST

Read this passage by the Scottish writer William McIlvanney.

My mother was a ferocious carer who had an almost mystical capacity to conjure solid worries out of air that to the rest of us looked untroubled and clear. Maybe somebody else was supposed to be with me and had gone out briefly.

I don't know. I am simply aware of myself there. The moment sits separate and vivid in my memory, without explanation, like a rootless flower. Whoever I was being, traveller or knight, I must have been tired. For I feel asleep.

Show how McIlvanney uses language to highlight his consciousness of being awake in those circumstances.

Language

Imagery

Language questions can involve imagery: **metaphor, personification, simile**. Each of these is a device of comparison, in which one thing is compared to another.

A metaphor is a figure of speech in which a word or phrase is applied to an object or action to which it is not literally applicable. For example:

> Arnold was a lion in the fight – just as a lion fights ferociously and bravely so Arnold fought fiercely and bravely.

In personification, an inanimate object is given the characteristics of a human being. For example:

> The sea was cruel that day – the sea is being compared to the human characteristic of cruelty.

Simile is the same as a metaphor but uses the words 'like' or 'as' and makes an explicit comparison. For example:

> Arnold was like a lion in the fight.

Read this passage for Question 1. This is taken from an article by the journalist Matthew Syed about professional football.

When we watch any Premier League match, we are witnessing players who have made it through a filtering process of staggering dimensions. It is a process that does not merely discard 98 per cent of those who aspire, but something closer to 99·9999 per cent. For every first-team player, there are millions of others, like grains of sand on the beach, who have tried, who have dreamt, but who have failed.

1 Show how the writer's use of imagery helps to make his argument clear.   **[2]**

The image is a simile – 'like grains of sand on a beach'. You can use the 'just as ... so' formula. Or you can analyse the image by pointing out that grains of sand look like each other and are indistinguishable, just like the unsuccessful footballers.

> *Just as there are millions of grains of sand on a beach* **[1]** *so there are huge numbers of hopefuls who do not succeed* **[1]**.

Read this paragraph for Question 2. This is taken from an article by Isabel Oakeshott about food production around the world.

My journey to expose the truth, to investigate the <u>dirty secret</u> about the way cheap food is produced, took me from the first mega-dairies and piggeries in Britain to factory farms in France, China, Mexico, and North and South America. I talked to people on the <u>front line</u> of the global food industry: <u>treadmill</u> farmers trying to produce more with less. I also talked to their neighbours – people experiencing the side effects of industrial farms. Many had stories about their homes <u>plummeting</u> in value, the desecration of lovely countryside, the disappearance of wildlife and serious health problems linked to pollution.

2 Analyse how imagery is used in this paragraph to convey the writer's criticism of industrial farming. **[2]**

> Possible answers include:
>
> - *'dirty secret': suggests that because they are appalling the methods used in factory farming are kept undisclosed* **[1]**
> - *'front line': is a reference to the battles that took place in the trenches and soldiers were killed, therefore industrial farming involves encounters with competitor, and the consequent losses* **[1]**
> - *'treadmill': suggests that farmers not only had to work hard, but their work was continuous, tedious and never ending* **[1]**
> - *'plummeting': suggests that the value of neighbouring homes dropped precipitously (sharply)* **[1]**

Questions

QUICK TEST
Read this passage. This is taken from an article by Carol Midgley on the attraction of shopping.

The pedestrianisation of city centres, though largely regarded as pro-citizen, is in fact primarily to maximise "footfall" and shoppers' "grazing time". This retail creep has ensured that increasingly there's not much else to do but shop. The more we consume, the less space there is to be anything other than consumers. The space to be citizens and make decisions equally and collectively about the world around us is diminished. It may be a free country, but we simply have the freedom to shop.

Show how the writer's use of imagery conveys her disapproval of the large amount of space that is now devoted to shopping.

Tone

When it comes to questions about **tone**, the actual tone will usually be obvious and easy to identify. Tone can be humorous, **sarcastic**, bitter, disapproving, sympathetic or positive.

Tone is created with a number of writing techniques, such as sentence structure, word choice, punctuation (especially parenthesis), imagery (including **hyperbole**) and contrast (especially with **juxtaposition** of formal and informal language).

When you are answering questions about tone, it sometimes helps to vocalise the text you are being questioned about in your head, so you listen to it without actually reading it aloud. This can help you be more aware of tone.

Read this passage for Question 1. This is taken from an article by Will Self about having to listen to music in public places.

Like all right-listening folk, I am an implacable enemy of all muzak. True, I'm not in the position of those factory workers in the 1940s and 1950s for whom muzak constituted a sort of mind control designed to move their tasks forward with its insistent and carefully calibrated tempo, while lulling them into the monotony of their tasks with its equally bland and repetitive melodies. However, even in modern Britain we are still subject to a form of control. I travel for work and there doesn't seem to be a hotel the length of the land that doesn't come equipped with its own piped sonic sewage, which is surely at least partially designed to send the punters quickly on their way.

1 Show how the writer uses language to convey his annoyance for muzak. **[2]**

Tone is a feature (and function) of language: look for word choice, imagery, sentence structure. You are asked to show how the tone of contempt is portrayed; the tone here is dismissive, scathing, critical, excoriating (severely critical), contemptuous; the short opening sentence is inverted, drawing attention to 'Like all right-listening folk' – establishing that, when it comes to muzak, like so many others, his abhorrence of it is 'right', as made clear by the climactic 'implacable enemy of muzak', revealing that he is an unrelenting adversary of 'muzak' (a term for background music played in shops, restaurants and hotels) – the word 'muzak' is pejorative – a useful word when dealing with tone, meaning contemptuous, critical, slighting, even insolent; 'implacable enemy' – 'implacable' means hostile and disapproving, conveying the adversarial tone of this short first sentence – strongly censorious (severely critical); the word choice 'mind control', suggests that muzak manipulates people, while 'lulling them into the monotony' suggests that muzak has an ulterior function of making people quietly compliant; 'piped sonic sewage' is a scathing description of the music played – the image is a metaphor comparing the way the sound of muzak is piped to public places with the way effluent is piped through sewers – a comparison that suggests the repulsive composition and sound of muzak; but note also the use of alliteration, where the combination of the plosive 'p' and the sibilant 's' sounds contribute to the foulness of the image; the last sentence is climactic, building up to the final expression 'where surely ... on their way', which is contemptuously mocking in tone, suggesting that 'punters' are driven away by the 'sonic sewage'.

Answers could include:

N5 The inversion used in the short opening sentence **[1]** draws attention to his claim that he is 'right-listening' **[1]**, establishing a tone of credibility **[1]**.

The climactic 'implacable enemy of muzak' **[1]** conveys a tone of contempt, showing his relentless adversarial attitude to 'muzak' **[1]**.

The last sentence is climactic **[1]**, building up to the final expression 'where surely ... on their way' **[1]**, which is contemptuously mocking **[1]** in tone, suggesting that 'punters are driven away by the 'sonic sewage'.

H The word choice 'lulling them into the monotony of their tasks' shows his contempt for the way muzak, even in previous decades, can be used to manipulate people into compliance, conveying his contempt for the practice **[1]**.

The metaphor 'piped sonic sewage' compares the way muzak is piped to public places with the way effluent is piped through sewers – a comparison that suggests the disgusting composition of muzak and thus his contempt **[2]**.

The use of alliteration in 'piped sonic sewage' combines the unpleasant plosive 'p' sound with the nasty 's' sound, thus contributing to his contempt for the foulness of 'muzak' **[1]**.

The climactic structure of the final sentence 'where surely ... on their way' reveals contempt for muzak by highlighting that 'punters' are driven away by the 'sonic sewage' **[1]**.

Questions

QUICK TEST

Read this passage. The extract is taken from an article by Carol Midgley on the attraction of shopping.

Well, that's just it. Turbo-consumerism – the age of instant gratification and voracious appetite for "stuff" – cannot make us happy and it never will. Every time we are seduced into buying one product, another appears that is "new", "improved", better than the one you have. Turbo-consumerism is the heroin of human happiness, reliant on the fact that our needs are never satisfied. A consumer society can't allow us to stop shopping and be content because then the whole system would die. Instead it has to sell us just enough to keep us going but never enough that our wants are satisfied. The brief high we feel is compensation for not having a richer, fuller life.

Show how the writer uses tone to convey her criticism of shopping.

Effectiveness

Effectiveness of an opening paragraph

In answering questions about the effectiveness of opening paragraphs, you need to think about how the writer has gone about attracting the reader's interest.

Look for:

- ways in which the writer addresses the reader – for example, does he/she use 'you'
- reference made to the subject matter of the passage (before you answer any question about the introduction you will have read the entire passage and will know the subject matter)
- any unusual, arresting or dramatic idea that would capture a reader's interest
- any unusual, arresting or dramatic use of language that would capture a reader's attention

Read the following introduction to an article about celebrities' use of Twitter:

> I'm not saying that Twitter celebs are fake, empty vessels who sociopathically toy with everyone in order to raise their profiles, but there are people who sometimes – actually, no, scrap the but; that's exactly what I'm saying.

1 Explain fully why the opening paragraph is an effective introduction. **[2]**

*The opening paragraph of this article is one sentence, which begins by stating what the writer is not saying and goes on, after the 'but', to state that 'that's exactly what I am saying'. Her use of 'I'm not saying that Twitter celebrities are fake' is, in fact, an effective rhetorical device (called **apophasis**) to capture readers' attention. Apophasis is a device whereby the writer actually does mention something by claiming that she is not going to mention it – in this case the phoniness of Twitter celebrities. After the 'but', which indicates a change in direction, she strengthens the point she claims she is not making by the use of 'sociopathically toy', an arresting image, implying that aspiring 'celebs' display extreme anti-social, insane characteristics as they 'toy' with people for their own ends in a highly manipulative way. But the main effect of the one long sentence is to create the impression that the writer is thinking as she writes, taking the reader with her – a kind of dramatic monologue with the reader as listener. The effect is reinforced by the use of the dash after 'sometimes' and the informal, almost colloquial tone of 'actually, no, scrap the but', which suggest a return to her original idea that these celebrities are 'fake, empty vessels'; the 'actually' and the parenthetical 'no' contribute to a new tone of decisiveness about her opinion of Twitter celebrities. The declarative after the semicolon – 'that's exactly what I am saying' – confirms the move from uncertainty ('I'm not saying') to the positive belief in her opinion, thereby preparing the way for the article itself.*

Possible answers include:

N5 The use of the 'I'm not saying' [1] is a device that allows her to mention that which she says she isn't going to mention [1].

H The use of apophasis (where a writer mentions something by saying that she isn't going to mention it) is Haggerty's way of talking about fake Twitter celebrities [1].

The use of punctuation after 'sometimes' – the dash and the parenthetical 'no' create the impression of the writer changing her mind as she thinks about her opinion as she writes [1].

Questions

QUICK TEST
Read the following introduction to an article about porridge by Karin Goodwin.

Oats, water, milk and salt: it was once a simple start to the Scottish day. But now even porridge is being given a full hipster makeover, with bowls complete with baked seasonal fruits, toasted seeds, chai spices, date syrup, bee pollen, and almond milk selling in metropolitan foodie haunts for £6 a pop.

Explain fully why the opening paragraph is an effective introduction.

Effectiveness

Effectiveness of conclusions

An effective conclusion can be the result of effective sentence structure or rhythm. Look for climax, repetition or tone used by the writer to create a memorable ending to the passage.

Pick an expression from the paragraph referred to in the question and show what it refers back to. This may be an earlier similar expression or an idea from earlier in the passage. There may be reference in the conclusion to a point made or expression used at the beginning of the passage that neatly rounds off or concludes the writer's argument or point of view.

Read the passage by Stephen Hawking on pages 5–7 to answer Questions 1 and 2.

1 Pick an expression from the last paragraph (lines 85–88) and say how it contributes to an effective conclusion to the passage. **[2]**

N5 The word choice 'dinosaur hunters' **[1]** refers back to the mention of dinosaurs in line 59 **[1]**, reminding the reader of one of the possible paradoxes and problems created by time travel.

Questions about conclusions in Higher need more sophisticated answers. Often you will be asked to 'evaluate' the conclusion, so you should say whether or not it is effective. Look for:

* a word or expression that signals summing up, such as 'clearly' or 'thus'
* the use of 'And' at the beginning of a sentence or paragraph – this signals the final point by isolating it in a sentence by itself
* climax – phrases or lists that dramatically keep the main point to the end
* any memorable phrase or idea
* an illustrative example of the ideas that have been discussed earlier in the passage
* reference to a phrase or idea that has been used earlier in the passage

2 How does the last sentence (lines 87–88) contribute to an effective conclusion to the passage? **[2]**

H The final sentence captures in one image two of the important aspects of the passage. It picks up on the remark about dinosaurs, creating a rounding-off effect **[1]**, but it also reminds us of the point that Hawking makes that history cannot be changed **[1]**.

You could refer to Hawking's use of language in creating a humorous tone at the end.

With the notion that both 'dinosaur hunters' (which don't exist) and 'historians' will be disappointed that time travel isn't going to happen, Hawking is clearly being playful [1] while at the same time making the serious point that history cannot be changed [1].

Questions

QUICK TEST
Read Passage 2 (*The big question*) on pages 8–9.
Evaluate the effectiveness of the last sentence as a conclusion to the passage.

'Evaluate' means that you can say that it is effective, or not effective, or partly effective, but you must give your reasons.

Summarising

Summarise a given number of points

Questions that ask you to summarise will state the number of points you should identify. Read the question carefully so that you are clear which kind of points you have to identify.

Underline as many relevant points as you can find and put the points into your own words.

At both N5 and Higher, if you are asked to summarise the differences between, say, A and B (worth 5 marks), you must list at least one point for each, then use any other permutation. Both A and B must be dealt with, but not necessarily equally.

This kind of question often appears as the last question in a section.

Read this passage for Question 1. This is taken from *How to build a time machine* by Stephen Hawking.

A wormhole is a theoretical 'tunnel' or shortcut, predicted by Einstein's theory of relativity, that links two places in space-time; it is where negative energy pulls space and time into the mouth of a tunnel, emerging in another universe. After all, nothing is flat or solid. If you look closely enough at anything you'll find holes and wrinkles in it. It's a basic physical principle, and it even applies to time. Something as smooth as a pool ball has tiny crevices, wrinkles and voids. Now it's easy to show that this is true in the first three dimensions. But trust me, it's also true of the fourth dimension. There are tiny crevices, wrinkles and voids in time. Down at the smallest of scales, smaller even than molecules, smaller than atoms, we get to a place called the quantum foam. This is where wormholes exist. Tiny tunnels or shortcuts through space and time constantly form, disappear, and reform within this quantum world. And they actually link two separate places and two different times.

Follow the procedure laid out above and list the points you have found. The number of marks allocated is an indication of the number of points you need to make.

1 Summarise the five main points that he makes. **[5]**

> Nothing is perfectly smooth or flat – everything is covered in holes or wrinkles **[1]**.
>
> It's easy to prove this fact in the dimensions of length, breadth and height **[1]**.
>
> Such wrinkles or holes also exist in time **[1]**.
>
> As we go smaller and smaller we eventually reach a place called quantum foam **[1]**.
>
> It's here that wormholes exist, linking separate places and different times **[1]**.

Read this passage for Question 2. This is taken from *The big question* by Steve Connor.

Two Russian mathematicians have suggested that the giant atom-smasher being built at the European centre for nuclear research, Cern, near Geneva, could create the conditions where it might be possible to travel backwards or forwards in time. In essence, Irina Aref'eva and Igor Volovich believe that the Large Hadron Collider at Cern might create tiny 'wormholes' in space which could allow some form of limited time travel.

Summarise the suggestions about time travel made by the Russian mathematicians, Irina Aref'eva and Igor Volovich. **[3]**

There are three points made by the Russian mathematicians:

- the giant atom-smasher at Cern might be able to produce the right environment to permit time travel **[1]**
- the Large Hadron Collider might produce 'wormholes' **[1]**
- such wormholes could allow some form of restricted travel backwards and forwards in time **[1]**

Questions

QUICK TEST
1. Read lines 16–29 of *The big question*.
Summarise the five main points that Brian Cox makes about time travel.
2. Read the penultimate paragraph of the same article (page 9).
Summarise the points made by John Gribbin.

Making comparisons

Comparing passages

H The Higher exam includes a question that involves a comparison of two passages. You need to read both passages and answer questions asking about comparisons between the two passages.

This question is worth 5 marks, or 16% of the marks available, so it is essential to know how to answer it properly. Questions will generally give the theme of both passages, laying out the concerns or ideas. You will be asked to identify where they agree or disagree. It is an ideas-based question, which has nothing to do with language analysis.

You will gain different marks for the way you answer the question:

* for 5 marks, you must identify comprehensively three or more key areas with full use of supporting evidence

* for 4 marks, you must identify clearly three or more key areas with supporting evidence

* for 3 marks, you must identify three or more key areas with relevant use of supporting evidence

To gain all 5 marks, then, you have to give precise evidence with a fully developed and detailed comment with comprehensive use of supporting evidence.

Follow these steps:

* identify areas of agreement or disagreement

* comment on and explain the evidence – your evidence can be in the form of quotations from the passages, or you can use bullet points

Read Passage 1 (pages 5–7) and Passage 2 (pages 8–9).

1 Look at both passages. The writers agree that time travel is impossible. Identify three key areas on which they agree. You should support the points by referring to important ideas in both passages. You may answer this question in continuous prose or in a series of developed bullet points.

You do not have to quote directly from the passage (though you can if you think that might be helpful), but you do have to show in what way your references to Passage 1 and Passage 2 support your key idea.

Key area 1: Einstein's theory of relativity allows for time travel into the past

Passage 1

Hawking points out that Einstein's theory of relativity predicted that wormholes or tunnels or shortcuts are possible, allowing travel through space and time.

Passage 2

Connor quotes Brian Cox of the University of Manchester: he claims that time travel into the past is theoretically possible according to Einstein's theory of relativity.

Key area 2: time travel may be possible using 'wormholes'

Passage 1

Hawking claims that where wormholes exist, and, with enough power and advanced technology, it might be possible to construct a giant wormhole that would allow time travel.

Passage 2

Connor says that a cosmologist suggested that it might be possible to manipulate a black hole to create a wormhole that would allow a time traveller to travel in an instant from one part of the universe to another and even back in time.

Key area 3: the problem of paradoxes

Passage 1

Hawking cites the problem with paradoxes: that though time travel back in time could create paradoxes, nevertheless the problem is actually the wormhole itself – as it expands it would create feedback which would ultimately destroy it.

Passage 2

Connor also cites the problem with paradoxes but claims that the physicist, John Gribbin, explains that even if we could create wormholes they would be so small that nothing could get through.

National 5 practice exam questions

Read Passage 1 *How to build a time machine*, by Stephen Hawking.

1. (a) Read lines 1–6. Explain why the first paragraph is an effective opening to the passage as a whole. **[2]**

    (b) Explain which word indicates to the reader that one of the three questions is the most significant. **[2]**

2. Read lines 7–16. Explain in your own words how, according to the writer, physicists regard time. **[3]**

3. Read lines 17–23. Identify three ways in which the writer makes the idea of time travel easier to understand. **[3]**

4. Read lines 31–45. Summarise the five stages Hawking outlines to explain what is meant by wormholes. **[5]**

5. Read lines 56–60. Explain in your own words what the writer means by what 'a time tunnel could do'. **[3]**

6. (a) Look at lines 61–70. Explain in your own words what, according to the writer, is the problem of paradoxes. **[4]**

    (b) Looking at these same lines, explain how the writer uses language to illustrate the problem. **[4]**

7. Explain how the two sentences in lines 79–80 provide a link at this stage in the writer's argument. **[2]**

8. Pick an expression from the final paragraph (lines 85–88) and show how it helps to contribute to an effective conclusion to the passage. You should refer to an expression or idea from earlier in the passage. **[2]**

How to answer the National 5 practice exam questions

1. (a) When there is an (a) and (b) question, the question is in two related parts.

    When answering questions about effective opening paragraphs:

    - look for anything that will engage the reader or address the reader directly, especially for the use of 'you'
    - look out for mention of the subject matter of the passage

    In this case, Hawking:

    - begins with the one-word minor sentence 'Hello', which is friendly and addresses the reader directly
    - tells the reader his name, and since it is one we recognise, our interest is engaged
    - mentions what is to be the subject matter of the passage – 'is time travel possible?'
    - uses questions to stimulate the reader's thoughts

    There are 2 marks, so you need to make two points.

    (b) The word that indicates the most important of the questions is 'ultimately'. You need to explain in what way the word is significant.

2. Underline the words in lines 7–16 that contain the answer. He makes four main points. You need to explain them.

3. He makes time travel easier to understand by referring the reader to sci-fi films in which the time traveller ends up in a different time era. You need to list these points.

4. 'Summarise' means identify the five stages and, as far as you can, put them into your own words.

5. You need to refer to the whole of the paragraph for the answer. Always pay attention to the line numbers since they will point you towards the answer. In this case, 3 marks = 3 points to be made.

6. (a) You need to make four points for 4 marks.

    (b) There is credit for each reference. Here you need to make two references, each with its own comment. You can use word choice and/or sentence structure to answer the question.

7. Remember the formula: quote then link back, quote and point forward. Here you are asked to show how it links the stages in the writer's argument.

8. Conclusion questions are straightforward – just follow the instruction.

Exam practice

Higher practice exam questions

Read Passage 3 *Forget Culloden: today's Highlanders have it made* by Rosemary Goring on this page and Passage 4, taken from *The Lion in the North* by John Prebble, on page 56.

Passage 3

Forget Culloden: today's Highlanders have it made

Rosemary Goring considers the full consequences down through the centuries of the Battle of Culloden, fought in 1746.

Culloden Moor is one of the bleakest places on the planet. I know, because I've been there. Wind-blasted, sodden, as featureless as a desert, it is made even more dismal thanks to the memory of the dreadful events that took place there on April 16, 1746. In less than an hour, King George II's men routed Bonnie
5 Prince Charlie's army, and sent those who evaded capture fleeing for their lives.

Those miserable events have been painted vividly on the national memory: the red coats with their smart tri-cornered hats and lethal muskets facing down a squad of kilted, porridge-scoffing Highlanders, brandishing targes˙ and broadswords that wouldn't have looked out of place in the Iron Age.

10 Nor is it an entirely erroneous picture. The Highlanders who rallied to the Jacobite cause would certainly have looked much as today's Taliban fighters do to British soldiers in Afghanistan. With their heavy plaids, Old Testament beards and couthy, woollen headgear, they would have presented a distinctly homespun picture. But appearances can be deceptive. Charles Edward Stuart's
15 men might not have been elegant, but in military terms they were far from hand-knitted.

So says Professor Murray Pittock of Glasgow University who has come upon evidence, while updating his book, *The Myth of the Jacobite Clans*, showing that this army was as sophisticated in weaponry as the Duke of
20 Cumberland's forces. Pittock believes the battle's outcome can be attributed not to an unfair struggle between swords and guns but to the Jacobites being outnumbered, the ground treacherous and the enemy's cannons better suited to the day than their own. As Pittock says: "Jacobites believed real soldiers used muskets – 2320 Jacobite muskets and 190 swords were picked
25 up from the battle-field. That's more than 10 to one."

You can almost understand why the Jacobites were portrayed as tribal warriors. Their political aims were supported only by a minority and threatened chaos,

if they won the day. More than that, though, the epithet of savage may
have been an attempt to reflect the barbarity of Culloden itself, one of the
30 grimmest and most ignominious battles in Scotland's long history of grim
and ignominious battles. Ragged, fierce, many not even speaking English,
this army was easy to caricature. But that doesn't fully explain it. Generation
after generation, Highlanders have been portrayed as dim-witted and hot-
tempered. The massacre of Glencoe, half a century before Culloden, horrified
35 genteel lowland society but the MacDonald clan was nevertheless depicted
as thrawn, cunning and fatally naive: in other words, authors of their own
misfortune.

From the earliest records, the Highlander was seen as backward and scary,
a creature apart from the rest of the race. And this cruel stereotype has
40 become a neat shorthand for city dwellers uneasy about their northern
compatriots, a feeling fuelled more by fear than by superiority. At least, if
there is a sense of superiority, it is utterly misplaced. In fact, I'd argue that
Highlanders are probably having the last laugh. Not only do they enjoy some
of the finest scenery in Europe, but as technology advances they are as well-
45 connected to the globe as those of us sweating away in polluted cities. That,
however, is the least of it. The canniest folk have realised the Highlands are
the best place to live because overnight the very things that once made the
Highlands so intimidating, and their people so alien, have become priceless.

In this ecologically stressed age – when pressure on fuel, water and space is
50 growing so fiercely it feels as if the walls and ceiling are closing in upon us –
the Highlands have an abundance of all these. Want to build an extension?
There'll be no quibble about finding a few extra square metres. Need to get
a turbine whirling? Wind is unlimited. Always wanted a stove in the living
room? There'll be peats aplenty to keep it alight. Worried a dry summer
55 could ruin the lawn? Drought won't be a problem; mud-slides, snow-melt
and flooding perhaps, but not hosepipe bans. But what about that blight
on the summer season that sees tour buses burning rubber as they flee the
Cairngorm sunset? Well, almost as many funds are being devoted to the
midge problem as to Heathrow's new runway. From traps and pesticides to
60 starvation, the Highlands' only true savage is under attack. And even if it
should remain resistant to science, the midge is migrating ever southwards.

So one day we may be looking north from beneath our West Lothian
mosquito nets, wondering why we didn't catch the last train to Pitlochry. I
could, of course, start talking about the values of community spirit, of the
65 enterprising can-do attitude of many Highland villagers, and the sense of
belonging that small towns in the middle of nowhere can bring. About what
a great place to bring up kids. But to do that would make me sound soft,
sentimental and southern, and if there's one thing that distinguishes the
Highlander, it's hardiness.

70 You can call that savage if you like. I prefer the word smart.

*targes – an archaic word for shield.

Passage 4

The Lion in the North

In this extract from his book, John Prebble describes the horrors of the Battle of Culloden and the real tragedy for the clans.

At dawn on Wednesday April 16, 1746, fewer than five thousand hungry and exhausted men limped into their battle-line on a bleak moor above Culloden House – clansmen, foothill tenantry, and a few newly arrived Irish and Franco-Scots. A gale was now driving sleet into their faces, and
5   they stood upon ground which no senior officer but Charles believed could be defended. Below on the Moray Firth to their left were English transports and men-of-war, and advancing toward them from Nairn were nine thousand men under the Duke of Cumberland, sixteen battalions of foot and another of militia, three regiments of horse and a company
10 of artillery. Three of the regular battalions were Lowland Scots, a fourth and the militia had been largely raised from Clan Campbell. Within an hour of noon the battle was over. Winnowed by Cumberland's guns, the clans at last charged through musketry and grapeshot, and where they could reach the enemy they slashed their way into three ranks of
15 levelled bayonets. Held back by volley-firing, Clan Donald did not engage the right of the red-coat line, and the men of Keppoch, Clanranald and Glengarry tore stones from the heathered earth and hurled them in impotent fury. The stubborn withdrawal from the charge became a hysterical rout, and the British marched forward to take ceremonial
20 possession of a victorious field, bayonetting the wounded before them, and cheering their fat young general. The long brawl of Scottish history had ended in the terrible blood of its best-remembered battle.

This time the policy of repression was inexorable. It began immediately with an order for the extermination of the wounded who still lay upon
25 the field. It was continued by the harsh imposition of martial law, the shooting and hanging of fugitives, the driving of stock, the burning of house and cottage. Lowland and English graziers came to Fort Augustus to buy the cattle driven in from the glens, and the Navy and the Army co-operated in a ruthless search for the fugitive prince, brutalizing those

30   who were thought to have information about him, and hanging a few
who would not give it.

In this sustained terrorization, Lowland regiments were as active as men
from English shires, and three officers long remembered for their bitter
cruelty were all Scots. The only government forces to show compassion
35   for the homeless and the hunted were the Campbell militia from Argyll.
The prisoners taken were tried in England, lest Scots juries be too faint-
hearted.

The axe was nobly busy on Tower Hill, and the gallows rope sang at
Carlisle, York, and Kennington Common. One hundred and twenty
40   common men were executed, a third of them deserters from the British
Army, but nearly seven hundred men, women and children died in
gaol or in the abominable holds of Tilbury hulks, from wounds, fever,
starvation or neglect. Two hundred were banished, and almost a
thousand were sold to the American plantations.

45   This time, too, the structure of the clan system was torn down and
left to its inevitable decay. The Clansmen were stripped of the tangible
manifestations of pride. When the proscription on Highland dress was
lifted in 1782, few of the common people accepted it. It became the
affection of their anglicized lairds, the fancy dress of the Lowlanders,
50   and the uniform of the King's Gaelic soldiers. The wearing of a red coat,
a belted plaid of black government tartan, enabled the young men of
the hills to keep some of their pride, and to follow the military example
of their ancestors. Their eagerness and their valour were prodigally
expended by successive governments. They were raised in the old way
55   of clan levies, each chief and his tacksmen bringing in so many of
their young tenants, by persuasion or by force. They were a unique and
splendid corps. Crime and cowardice were rare, and when they mutinied,
as they sometimes did, it was with dignity and because the promises
made to them by their chiefs had been broken by the government.

60   The last tragedy of the clans may not be the slaughter of Culloden, but
the purchase and wasteful expenditure of their courage by the southern
peoples who had at last conquered them.

Higher practice exam questions

1. Read lines 1–5 of Passage 3.

    (a) Explain in your own words two reasons that the writer gives for thinking that Culloden Moor is 'one of the bleakest places on the planet'. **[2]**

    (b) Read the third sentence (lines 2–4) and show how her use of language reinforces her opinion of Culloden Moor. You should refer to sentence structure and word choice. **[4]**

2. Read lines 6–9. Show how the writer's use of language conveys her opinion that the events that took place there were miserable. **[4]**

3. Read lines 17–25. In your own words, explain Professor Murray Pittock's reasons for the Jacobite failure. **[3]**

4. Read lines 31–36. By referring to at least two examples, analyse how the writer uses language to present the ways in which Highlanders have been portrayed. **[4]**

5. Show how the paragraph between lines 37 and 40 performs a linking function at this stage in the writer's argument. **[2]**

6. Read lines 48–55 ('In this ecologically stressed age … hosepipe bans'). Show how the writer's use of language conveys a more attractive picture of the Highlands. **[4]**

7. Evaluate the effectiveness of the final paragraph as a conclusion to the passage. **[2]**

Questions on both Passage 3 and Passage 4.

8. Look at both passages.

    Both writers agree about the Battle of Culloden and its aftermath.

    Identify three key areas on which they agree.

    You should support the points by referring to important ideas in both passages.

    You may answer this question in continuous prose or in a series of developed bullet points. **[5]**

How to answer the Higher practice exam questions

1. (a) Questions in parts (a) and (b) format are related. You should read both (a) and (b) before beginning to answer. Part (a) is a straightforward question, testing your ability to read carefully and to be able to express yourself succinctly.

   (b) This is a language question with 4 marks. You are instructed to use sentence structure and word choice. You need two sentence structure references + comment and two word choice references + comment. If you provide only one reference, then you need to ensure that your comment is developed. There are many possibilities, especially for word choice.

2. You can use sentence structure, word choice, imagery, tone, punctuation, contrast – whichever you feel most comfortable using. You need four references + comment or fewer references but with more developed comments. For the sake of clarity you should try to answer in bullet points.

3. There are 3 marks, so you need three points.

4. Read the question carefully. The question is about the way Highlanders have been presented and not about the battle itself.

5. The question asks you to look at the entire paragraph. Note 'at this stage in the writer's argument' means pay attention to the linking of stages, not just paragraphs.

6. This is another language question with 4 marks.

7. You can answer this best by referring to language and ideas.

8. You need to look for three key areas of agreement. Just to write down three such ideas will gain you 3 marks out of 5. You then need to support your choice of ideas with reference to the passages.

Grammar

Knowing how sentences are put together is an essential skill when it comes to answering questions in the RUAE and Critical Reading papers. Developing these language skills help you when it comess to analysing prose fiction and non-fiction, plays and poems. Knowledge about grammar will also help you develop your own writing abilities.

Establishing meaning

We need to work out how meaning is established in English.
Meaning has everything to do with **word order**.

Word order

Take the following sentence:

Alison loves Andrew.

Now let's change the word order:

Andrew loves Alison.

Do these two sentences still mean the same thing?

It's even more obvious if we alter:

Kevin loves tennis.   to   Tennis loves Kevin.

Meaning in English is dependent on word order. Change the word order and you change the meaning. Here is another example:

I swam across the stream slowly.

Now shift the word *slowly* to the beginning of the sentence:

Slowly, I swam across the stream.

Even by shifting the position of one word, we have changed the meaning! By placing the word 'slowly' at the beginning, we now draw attention to how the swimmer swam across the stream – the swimmer swam slowly, he swam in an unhurried manner, and by placing the word at the beginning of the sentence we are drawing attention to that fact.

It's really important to understand that word order – the structure of a sentence – is what conveys meaning. Change the structure and you change the meaning. You should remember that when you are writing as well as reading!

Sentences

In order to read, understand and analyse, you need to know how sentences are put together. To do this, you need to be able to analyse and evaluate the effects that writers can create by their use of sentence structure.

Many of the questions in the N5 and Higher RUAE papers are about the analysis and the effects of various kinds of sentence structure. It is essential to understand how sentences are put together.

Sentences are made up of four levels:

sentences

clauses

word groups

words

Sentences can consist of one or more clauses. Clauses consist of one or more word groups, and these word groups consist of one or more words. You have to know about the functions of individual words. We will take these in reverse order, starting with words.

Words and word classes

You should know about words such as nouns, verbs, adjectives, adverbs, prepositions and pronouns. We refer to these as **word classes**.

The tables show most of the word classes you will come across in your reading – noun, verb, adjective and so on.

Nouns	Example	Function
Concrete noun	boy, girl, man, dog, couch, supermarket, loch, television, smartphone	A noun is the name of something. Concrete nouns are recognised by your five senses – you can see, hear, smell, taste or touch them.
Proper noun	Fiona, George, Queen Elizabeth, New York, Scotland, Tess	Names of people and places. Proper nouns should always have capital letters (upper case).
Abstract nouns	happiness, sadness, tiredness, nosiness, kingdom, freedom, excitement, merriment, beauty, truth	The name of an emotion or a feeling – something that you cannot touch. Abstract nouns often end in *-ness*, *-dom* or *-ment*.
Personal pronouns	I, you (singular), he, she, it, we, you (plural), they, them	A word which stands for a noun.

Nouns	Example	Function
Possessive pronouns	my, your, his, hers, its, our, your, their, mine, ours, yours, theirs	Indicates belonging.
Reflexive pronouns	myself, yourself, himself, herself, itself, ourselves, yourselves, themselves	Used in reflexive verbs, such as *I am washing myself. Watch you don't cut yourself! He is buying himself that book.*
Relative pronouns	who, whom, whose, which, that, as	That is the man **who** walked here; that is the woman **whose** house has been bought; that is the snake **which** escaped; here is the wall **that** Jack built; such people **as** those make good teachers.

Verbs and adverbs	Example	Function
Verbs	To skip, to jump, to sing, to read, to play – all doing words. To be, to exist, to have – all state of being verbs.	Traditionally known as a *doing word*, though many verbs indicate a state of being.
Adverbs	sadly, incautiously, mostly, however, furthermore, slowly, speedily, determinedly	An adverb modifies a verb. Adverbs often end in *-ly*. They usually answer questions such as *why*, *when* or *how*. *Then*, *however* and *moreover* are also adverbs.
Prepositions	the book is *on* the table; the cat is *under* the bed; the idea was *in* his head	Prepositions indicate relationships between objects or words.
Prepositional phrases	The workers *on the railway line* could see *at first glance* the approaching train. *in the morning; down the motorway; at the cinema; beside the coffee machine; under the train*	Phrases usually have an adverbial function, modifying verbs or nouns. In the example on the left, the phrase *on the railway line* modifies *the workers* and *at first glance* modifies the verb *see*.

Adjectives and related words	Example	Function
Adjectives	beautiful, excited, sad, clever, intelligent, blue, red, yellow, four, difficult	A word that describes things or people – adjectives modify/describe meaning.
Comparative and superlative adjectives	good, better, best; bad, worse, worst; happy, happier, happiest; beautiful, more beautiful, most beautiful	Comparative adjectives compare differences between two nouns. Superlative adjectives compare differences between three or more nouns.
Demonstrative adjective (sometimes referred to as determiners)	this top is prettier than that one over there; all these dogs are very clever	Demonstrative adjectives refer to something already mentioned, indicating which top and which dogs are being talked about.
Definite article (also a determiner, i.e. has an adjectival function)	The word *the* is the definite article.	The definite article modifies or restricts meaning: hence the difference between cat and the cat, so that the listener or reader knows which cat is being referred to.
Indefinite article (also a determiner, i.e. has an adjectival function)	a book, a shop, an apple, an adventure, an orange	The words *a* and *an* are indefinite articles.

Word class	Example	Function
Conjunctions	and, because, or, since, but, yet	Linking or joining words.
Interjections	Hark! Hush! Alas! Bravo! Eh?	Words and sounds used to attract attention or to express emotion or surprise. Interjections can have a dramatic effect.

Every word in a sentence belongs to one of these word classes. You need to be able to identify the word classes so that you can work out the functions of words in a sentence.

For example:

The boy crossed the road.

- *The* is a **definite article**. It is a determiner indicating which boy we are talking about – it was *the* boy as opposed to *a* boy.
- *boy* is a **noun**.
- *crossed* is a **verb**. It is the 'doing word'.
- *the* is another **definite article**.
- *road* is a **noun**.

Word groups

Sentences also consist of word groups. For example:

His mobile phone rang at eleven o'clock in the morning.

You should recognise that *rang* in the sentence above is the verb. (Remember a verb is a doing word.) Once you have identified the verb, you are left with three word groups:

1   His mobile phone

2   at eleven o'clock

3   in the morning.

Group 1 is a **nominal** (or noun) group because it has the function of a noun.

Groups 2 and 3 are **prepositional phrases**. You must be able to recognise prepositional phrases (see the tables above). In the sentence above, the prepositional phrases are in their 'normal' place. If we move them, the meaning of the sentence is changed:

In the morning, at eleven o'clock, his mobile phone rang.

By shifting the prepositional phrases *In the morning* and *at eleven o'clock* to the beginning of the sentence, we have highlighted their meaning, drawing attention to *when* the phone rang. By placing them at the beginning of the sentence, the writer has given these phrases emphasis.

The shifting of prepostional phrases is more common than you might think. You need to look out for this language device in your reading, and you should use this technique in your own writing.

Clause structure

The next level up from word groups is clause structure. A clause is a unit that contains a subject and a main verb. A clause can also contain an object and/or modifier. For example:

The dog jumped over the burn.

The main verb is *jumped*. Therefore it's a sentence that consists of one clause, a main clause, and we know it is a main clause because it stands by itself and makes sense.

Not all parts of a verb make up a main verb. The infinitive doesn't count as a main verb. The infinitive is that part of the verb with to in front of it: to speak, to run, to jump, to swim. For example:

I like to run every morning.

The main verb is *like*. Since *to run* is the infinitive, it doesn't count as a main verb, so there is only one clause.

There are also other parts of the verb that don't make up a main verb, such as those parts that end in *-ing*: *walking, jumping, swimming, gardening, writing*. These are **present participles**. For example:

Harry walked to school eating an apple.

The present participle *eating* is not a main verb. The main verb in the sentence is *walked*. The sentence is made up of only one clause.

Sentences are usually made up of one or more clauses, which are made up of word groups, which in turn consist of words. When it comes to answering questions about sentence structure (or about other language features), considering all four levels will help you answer questions about language.

Sentences

A sentence can consist of a main clause and/or a subordinate clause. If a sentence contains only a main clause, it is called a **simple** sentence. For example:

The boy ate the apple.

If a sentence contains a main clause and a subordinate clause, it is a **complex** sentence.

In the following sentence, there are two main verbs: *jumped* and *flowed*, so there are two clauses. You can use two vertical lines to separate the clauses:

The dog jumped over the burn, | | which flowed through the garden.

The first clause *The dog jumped over the burn* is a main clause because it can stand on its own and make sense.

The second clause *which flowed through the garden* does not make sense on its own. It is therefore a subordinate clause. It needs the main clause in order to make sense.

Use the labels MC for the main clause and SC for the subordinate clause SC:

                MC   SC

The dog jumped over the burn, | | which flowed through the garden.

For example:

The ship sank in the harbour after it had been struck by a submarine.

There are two main verbs, so there are two clauses:

- *The ship sank in the harbour* (main clause)
- *after it had been struck by a submarine* (subordinate clause)

So we can use the labels MC and SC:

                MC   SC

The ship sank in the harbour | | after it had been struck by a submarine.

These sentences contain a main clause and a subordinate clause so they are called **complex sentences**.

As you saw on page 60, changing the word order in a sentence affects the meaning of the sentence. For example:

              MC   SC

I always turn off my phone | | when I arrive at school.

If the subordinate clause is moved to the beginning of the sentence, you get:

              SC   MC

When I arrive at school, | | I always turn off my phone.

In this version, attention is drawn to *when* and *where* the phone is turned off. The clauses have been *inverted* and the meaning is affected. This sentence structure is called **inversion**.

Inversion isn't always about moving a clause. It can also involve moving a phrase (usually a prepositional phrase, with the function of an adverb). For example:

The newly painted ship sailed down the Clyde on a beautiful May morning.

There are two prepositional phrases in that sentence:

- *down the Clyde*
- *on a beautiful May morning*

Both are adverbial. The first phrase tells you *where* the ship sailed. The second phrase tells you *when* it sailed.

If one of the prepositional phrases is shifted to the beginning of the sentence then attention is drawn to it:

> Down the Clyde, the newly painted ship sailed on a beautiful May morning.

We have now drawn attention to the *where*, stressing that it was down the Clyde that the ship sailed.

Alternatively, you can draw attention to the *when*:

> On a beautiful May morning, the newly painted ship sailed down the Clyde.

Or you can stress both the *where* and the *when*:

> Down the Clyde, on a beautiful May morning, the newly painted ship sailed.

The last sentence sounds a touch poetic, but it does attract the reader's attention.

Types of sentence

There are five types of sentences.

- **Simple** sentences contain one main clause.
- **Complex** sentences contain a main clause and one or more subordinate clauses.
- **Compound** sentences contain two or more main clauses joined by a conjunction. For example:

> The lightning flashed, and the thunder rolled.

- **Compound-complex** sentences contain two or more main clauses with at least one subordinate clause. For example:

> The lightning flashed, and the thunder rolled, after which the rain fell in torrents.

- **Minor** sentences are sentences without a main verb. For example:

> She was pointing to the roof where the sniper lay. An informer.
>
> (*The Sniper* by Liam O'Flaherty)

'*An informer*' is a minor sentence. The effect of this short, minor sentence is highly dramatic, drawing attention to the woman who gives away the sniper's position. It isolates the information and makes it highly immediate.

Features and effects of sentence structure

Sentences can be structured in many different ways. Different types of sentence structure can be used for particular effects.

Use of inversion, including climax

Inversion is used to shift emphasis. For example:

> When the organisers of the 2015 Super Bowl were looking for someone to follow in the footsteps of Diana Ross and Whitney Houston and belt out The Star-Spangled Banner in front of a global audience of 160 million, it's not hard to see why they chose Idina Menzel.
>
> (Ed Potton, *The Times*, 6 February 2015)

This long sentence has been inverted. The main clause, *it's not hard to see why they chose Idina Menzel*, comes at the end. The writer has chosen to place the subordinate clause, *when the organisers*, at the beginning. This delays the main clause to the end of the sentence and creates a climax.

The delay of the main clause to the end is also created by the insertion of phrases such as

When the organisers of the 2015 Super Bowl
to follow in the footsteps of Diana Ross and Whitney Houston
belt out The Star-Spangled Banner
in front of a global audience.

The cumulative effect of these phrases is to delay the climax, *why they chose Idina Menzel*, highlighting the significance of choosing the star of *Frozen*.

Another use of inversion is shown here:

> When the first zoo visitors arrived, the ape began to enthusiastically hurl his missiles at the gawping humans.
>
> (Steve Connor, *The Independent*, August 2011)

The main clause has been placed at the end of the sentence. This draws attention to the main clause and creates climax. The climactic point isn't so much the ape throwing missiles, but is the silly humans who just stand there mesmerised.

Climax is more common than you might think. Always look for climax and know how to show how it has been created and comment on the point highlighted by it.

Choice of words or phrases at the beginning of sentences

There can be two main effects of placing particular words or phrases at the beginning of sentences:

- the technique draws attention to the words and phrases, thus highlighting meaning
- it delays the main point to the end of the sentence, thus creating climax

For example:

> Red of face, only half awake, the left eye partly closed,
> the right staring stupid and glassy, he stared at the map.
>
> *(Lord Jim* by Joseph Conrad)

The phrases

Red of face
only half awake
the left eye partly closed
the right staring stupid and glassy

by being placed at the beginning of the sentence, draw attention to the man's overwhelming tiredness.

The writer has also created climax by putting all these phrases before the main point, *he stared at the map*. This draws attention to the difficulties that the subject of the sentence has dealing with reading the map.

Glossary

Adverb – an adverb or adverbial phrase modifies (alters) mainly a verb, though an adverb can modify an adjective, another adverb or even a whole sentence. Adverbs typically express time (when), place (where), manner (how), frequency (how often) or degree (to what extent). Remember, though, that adverbs used as connectors – however, otherwise, thus, meanwhile, therefore, additionally (there are many more) – don't usually follow a comma, only a semi-colon.

Anaphora – the repetition of words or phrases at the beginning of sentences or clauses to intensify the point being made (also known as parallel structure).

Climax – very often sentences are structured so that the main point comes at the end, thus creating climax; there is a build-up, using phrases to delay that main point to the end.

Colloquialism – vocabulary which is informal, like everyday speech and even slang. Often used for humour or to make a passage seem real.

Cumulative intensification – usually associated with lists, including **tricolon**, where a series of items increase in degree, each point greater than the previous.

Definite article – the word 'the'.

Demonstrative adjective – 'this', 'that', 'these', 'those' – used to indicate which objects/ideas are being referred to, called a referent; they are also used to help distinguish one object or idea from another.

Hyperbole – gross exaggeration; can have a humorous effect.

Incremental intensification – similar to cumulative intensification; a list that increases the point being made by degrees.

Indefinite articles – the words 'a' and 'an'.

Inversion – where the normal word order of a sentence has been inverted, i.e. the subordinate clause precedes the main clause: Although it was cold that night, I still went swimming'.

Irony – bringing together of two words, ideas or even objects so that a contrast is implied and each comments on the other; involves contrasts or opposites, often stating the opposite of what is actually meant, but not always for humorous reasons and not necessarily to ridicule.

Juxtaposition – placing side by side of two objects, ideas or words, usually to make contrast clear.

Metaphor – a device of comparison in which a word or phrase is applied to an object or action to which it is not literally applicable.

Parenthesis – adds information that illustrates the points being made, using brackets, dashes or commas.

Pejorative – a useful word attaching criticism to a normally neutral term: words such as ambitious, clever and working class can all be used pejoratively, depending on the tone with which they are used.

Personal pronouns – words such as I, you, he, she, it, we, you (plural) or they; pronouns that refer to someone already mentioned, where identity is clear.

Personification – ascribing human qualities to inanimate objects; another form of metaphor.

Prepositions – indicate relationships between objects, ideas or parts of sentences: by, with, to, from, under, below, in front of, on.

Prepositional phrase – usually a phrase followed by a noun group or an object: on the table, in the morning, on the motorway, inside the ship, in my head; they are adverbial and can modify adjectives, other adverbs and whole sentences.

Register – the appropriateness of language for a given context, from colloquial (more like spoken English) to formal (the language of formal writing).

Repetition – points, phrases or words that are repeated in order to intensify the point being made.

Rhetorical question – a question that implies its own answer; it is usually used as a device to underline or clarify a point being made by the writer (or speaker).

Sarcasm – stating the opposite of what you mean in order to mock or ridicule.

Short sentences – when a short sentence follows a long sentence, the short sentence will be blunt and dramatic. Short sentences on their own make the point briefly and bluntly or sharply.

Simile – a device of comparison that uses 'like' or 'as'.

Symbolism – a device of representation, used to reveal something or an idea of significance.

Tense – a way of expressing time; there are three main tenses in English: simple present (I jump), simple past (I jumped) and simple future (I shall/will jump).

Tone – the style in which something is written (or spoken), i.e. friendly, sarcastic, appeasing or angry.

Transpose – to switch, move or alter position of something.

Tricolon – a list containing three items. Tricolon is a very effective rhetorical device that gives weight to each item while the rhythm created contributes to a climactic build-up, highlighting the last item.

Answers

Quick test – answers

By the use of the short, declarative sentence the writer conveys exasperation that cows live such a curtailed life.
By the use of inversion, the writer draws attention to the phrase 'they never see grass', expressing condemnation of the artificial life that cows are forced to live.

Page 13 Quick Test

1. The 'hoes and ploughshares' reveal an early agricultural community; 'chisels and saws' reveal the prior presence of woodworkers; 'forgotten gods' reveal a pre-Christian community; 'scalpels and spatulas' suggest an early surgical unit; and the collection of '48 human skulls' suggests a storage facility for severed heads.
2. The rivers were either redirected away from houses or they were dug deep beneath residential properties in subterranean routes.

Page 15 Quick Test

1. They formed a tightly knit group which enormously benefited Glasgow's financial development.
2. The Chinese helped Glaswegians develop a more sophisticated sense of taste in food.
3. There weren't many of them and they were country dwellers from deprived areas.

Page 17 Quick Test

1. The conjunction 'But' indicates a link between the previous point and the point about to be made. It also suggests a change in the direction of the argument from the previous ideas about physical length to the ideas prompted by 'length in time', which Hawking is about to explore.
2. The phrase 'This kind of time machine' refers back to the time machines that travel through wormholes, as discussed in the previous paragraph. The phrase 'fundamental rule that governs the entire universe' anticipates the idea that Hawking is going on to develop, that cause always precedes effect.

Page 19 Quick Test

1. Answers could include:
   N5 'manages to triumph over' – suggests that he overcomes the shackles that trap modern man.
   'indeed, harness' – suggests that he can control to his advantage the restrictions that modern man suffers.
   H 'a hero *in spite of* modernity' – the italics stress the fact that his heroic existence challenges modernity and that he benefits from confronting it in his own way.
   'gelded appendages' – suggests that most modern men have become emasculated by work pressures on them and Bond is just the opposite: he revels in freedom.
2. Answers could include:
   'manages to triumph over' – suggests his ability to overcome everything that emasculates contemporary man.
   'indeed, harness' – suggests that he can use to his advantage the very technology that makes men today so drab.

Page 21 Quick Test

1. The use of inversion places the main point of the sentence – the abundance of trees and the perfect air – at the end to draw attention to the attractiveness of the place.
2. The writer uses climax in this sentence, highlighting the amount of milk produced.
3. Answers could include:

Page 23 Quick Test

N5 1. The use of the list – 'racist, reactionary, bigoted small-town America' – conveys how backward and provincial some areas of the USA were in the 1960s.
H 2. The tricolon 'goodness, sincerity and generosity', where the increasing number of syllables in each word builds up to the climax 'generosity', reveals the variety of qualities and decencies possessed by the boxer.

Page 25 Quick Test

N5 1. The writer uses inversion to delay the main point: being in a bookshop and surprisingly looking for a cat.
H 2. By her use of inversion, the writer delays her main point to the end of the sentence, thereby making clear where her real quarrel lies – with the marketing of books; there is, though, an element of apophasis in the use of the inversion: by stating that the *real* quarrel is *not* with the quality of the writing, there is an implication that the writing is part of her quarrel; the adjective *real* perhaps suggesting that there is a quarrel with the writing, though it is slightly less significant.

Page 27 Quick Test

N5 1. 'seized every opportunity' – suggests that he has great respect for their positive attitudes.
H 'seized every opportunity' – suggests that he has much respect for their eagerness to take every available chance to overcome the pressure.
N5 2. 'facing up to them' – suggests that they will let nothing faze them.
H 'facing up to them' – suggests that they will meet their problems unflinchingly and turn them into opportunities.
3. The writer's use of the repetition of the imperative (the use of the command 'Don't') creates a cumulative intensification of her annoyance and frustration at the demands made by the 'army of professionals'.

Page 29 Quick Test

N5 By placing the phrases 'Down at the smallest of scales', 'smaller even than molecules' and 'smaller than atoms' at the beginning of the sentence, Hawking highlights the fact that he is impressed by the smallness of quantum foam.
H Hawking conveys how impressed he is by the sheer tiny size of quantum foam by placing the phrases 'Down at the smallest of scales', 'smaller even than molecules' and 'smaller than atoms' at the beginning of the sentence, emphasising the diminutive size of the quantum foam.

Page 31 Quick Test

The short three-word monosyllabic sentence – 'I don't know' – comes at the beginning of a new paragraph, creating a contrast with the previous paragraph's longer sentences in which he expresses his uncertainty of being alone and drawing attention to and dramatically reinforcing the fact that he simply does not know why he is alone.

Page 33 Quick Test

N5 In the paragraph, the writer asks four questions, each of which expresses her concerns about the point of shopping.
H Throughout the paragraph, the writer asks four questions, which range from the first question expressing her doubts about how shopping is taking over lives – implying a criticism of shopping – to questioning if it's really such a bad thing in the final question, which implies that it seems all right just to let people get on with it.

Page 35 Quick Test

The colon after the word 'priceless' signals an explanation of the term that trees are nature's way of measuring times past.

Page 37 Quick Test

Answers could include:

' such as smoked salmon,' provides additional information about the kind of example of what were once expensive foods.

' – 50 billion of them a year worldwide – ' provides additional information about the sheer number of industrially reared animals.

Page 39 Quick Test

McIlvanney uses tense to reinforce the awareness that he was of being awake. He switches from the past tense of the first paragraph ('I fell asleep') to the present tense of 'I don't now' and 'I am simply aware of myself there', creating an immediacy of wakefulness.

Page 41 Quick Test

Possible answers include:

* 'grazing time' – suggests by the image of 'grazing' that shoppers are like sheep, an animal noted for its predisposition to follow and not noted for its intelligence
* 'retail creep' – just as 'creep' suggests a slow, steady, stealthy movement not intended to be noticed, so the pedestrianisation of city centres has been done gradually but imperceptibly
* 'creep' has strong **pejorative** tones, suggesting underhand and likely to destroy

Page 43 Quick Test

The use of inverted commas round '"stuff"' indicates she is being sarcastic, that she doesn't care about products and goods. She regards them as not worthy of description; "stuff" is being used in an insulting way.

The phrase 'the heroin of human happiness' shows the author's disapproval by metaphorically comparing shopping to taking heroin, a highly addictive drug that can be fatal, but by developing the metaphor, she sharpens her criticism by suggesting that, like the effect of heroin, the happiness we get from shopping can never be satisfied – we always want more.

Page 45 Quick Test

• It introduces the reader to the subject matter – the updating of porridge for current times.

• It explains what 'makeover' for porridge involves.

• It begins with a list of ingredients for making traditional porridge.

• The colon introduces a comment on the list.

• Note the alliteration of the 's' sound after the colon.

• Note use of current, fashionable **register** – 'hipster', 'makeover' – to appeal to 'trendy' reader.

• List of fashionable, very modern products – 'chai spices', 'bee pollen' – again to appeal to young, trendy reader.

• The expression 'metropolitan foodie haunts for £6 a pop' conveys a sarcastic tone, suggesting the writer isn't taking updated porridge too seriously.

Page 47 Quick Test

Possible answers include:

The single sentence paragraph draws attention to the writer's opinion that time travel could happen.

The paragraph is isolated, drawing attention to the writer's point that time travel may be possible.

The sentence repeats the word 'crazy', giving a humorous tone, effectively concluding the passage.

Page 49 Quick Test

1. It could be that time travel is possible, but most likely it won't happen.

Time travel back in time will not happen.

Time travel into the future might occur.

Einstein's theory of relativity might allow time travel into the past.

Most scientists rule it out.

2. The LHC could produce a wormhole by accident.

Such a wormhole would be very tiny.

Nothing would be able to travel through it.

It's unlikely that anyone could visit from outer space.

It's not entirely inconceivable.

N5 exam practice – answers

1. (a) Possible answers include:
   The use of the one-word minor sentence as the first word of the passage is friendly and appealing [1].
   The fact that he uses his name is as though he is speaking directly to the reader [1].
   The question 'is time travel possible?' identifies the subject matter of the passage [1].
   (b) The word 'ultimately' [1] indicates that the final question is the most important because it suggests that the very final stage is to deal with the laws of nature in order to control time [1].

2. Possible answers include:
   Physicists regard time as a fourth dimension after width, height and length [1].
   Some material substances last longer than others [1].
   Everything, then, extends in time as well as space [1].

3. He makes time travel easier to understand by using the analogy of sci-fi movies [1].
   The huge time machines in these movies pass through time tunnels [1].
   The time traveller ends up in a different time period [1].

4. Nothing is smooth or flat – everything is covered in holes or wrinkles [1].
   It's easy to see these holes/wrinkles in the three dimensions of length, breadth and height [1].
   Such holes/wrinkles exist in time [1].
   As matter gets smaller and smaller we get to a place called quantum foam [1].
   It's at this place that wormholes exist, linking separate places and separate times [1].

5. A time tunnel could take travellers to other planets [1].
   A time tunnel could also take the traveller back to the same place [1], but at an earlier time, even millions of years previously [1].

6. (a) Time tunnels take travellers back into the past, even by a minute [1]. The traveller then meets his former self, a minute previously [1]. That man would no longer exist [1]. He could no longer return to the present – which is obviously impossible [1].
   (b) Possible answers include:
   The use of the colon in line 61 signals Hawking's explanation of the 'problem of paradoxes' – he says that the problem provides fun. (1 mark for reference to line 61 + 1 mark for comment)
   The two questions in lines 67–69 make clear, with their brief answers, the impossibility of such a situation arising. The question 'Who fired the shot?' [1] clarifies the impossibility of the situation since he will no longer exist to be able to go back in time to fire the shot in the first place [1].
   'Mad Scientist paradox' – suggests that paradoxes are not to be taken seriously. (1 mark for reference + 1 for comment)

7. 'I think a wormhole like this' refers back to the point he has been making about the problems wormholes pose in terms of impossibilities [1], and 'feedback' indicates that he going to explain the problem in terms of feedback [1].

8. Possible answers include:
   The word choice 'dinosaur hunters' [1] recalls the mention of dinosaurs in line 59 [1].
   The final sentence with the balance of 'disappointment for dinosaur hunters' and 'a relief for historians' [1] creates a rhythmic and humorous tone, in keeping with the writer's wry humour throughout [1].

Higher exam practice – answers

1. (a) Because it reminds us of the battle that took place there **[1]**. It is as uninspiring as any wasteland **[1]**.
   (b) Possible word choice answers include:
   'Wind-blasted' – suggests by the use of 'blasted' that the wind has blown with such force that it demolishes anything in its path **[1]**.
   'sodden' – suggests that the rain is so heavy that it leaves everything drenched and soaked through **[1]**.
   Possible sentence structure answers include:
   The pile-up of adjectives at the beginning of the third sentence delays the point about the battle to the end, thus highlighting it as the worst aspect of the Moor **[1]**.
   The climax of the last sentence of the paragraph emphasises that many of Charlie's army were sent 'fleeing for their lives' in order to escape death **[1]**.

2. Possible answers include:
   The use of the colon at the end of line 6 signalling the expansion and explanation of what the writer means by 'miserable events' **[1]**.
   The explanation is in the form of a list within a list, illustrating the range and extent of the obstacles faced by the Highlanders **[1]**.
   The word choice 'lethal muskets' suggests that the red coats' weapons were modern and deadly **[1]**.
   They were more than a match for 'a squad of kilted, porridge-scoffing Highlanders', suggesting their primitive appearance **[1]**.
   The word 'squad' suggests a mere group or gang, not a professional army **[1]**.
   That they were 'brandishing targes and broadswords' suggests a picture of mediaeval fighters who couldn't survive the 'lethal weapons' of the enemy **[1]**.
   The whole sentence is climactic, building up by means of the lists to 'wouldn't have looked out of place in the Iron Age' **[1]**.
   The climax highlights a primitive fighting force that could so easily be defeated – all building a picture of the 'miserable events' **[1]**.
   Any four of the above list.

3. Possible answers include these three main reasons:
   • there were more redcoats than rebels **[1]**
   • the battle ground was dangerous and hostile **[1]**
   • the redcoats' weaponry (ordnance) was more appropriate given the conditions that day **[1]**

4. Possible sentence structure answers include:
   The sentence in line 31 'Ragged … caricature' uses inversion, where the main point is placed at the end, emphasising that they looked like easily mocked stereotypes, a parody of themselves **[1]**.
   Possible word choice answers include:
   'many not even speaking English' suggests their parochial (and, by implication, unsophisticated) background **[1]**.
   'thrawn' is a Scots word meaning stubborn, uncooperative or awkward, and suggests here that they were unimaginative. Its tone is pejorative, suggesting lacking in common sense **[1]**.
   'cunning' in this context suggests crafty and deceitful **[1]**.

5. The clause 'From the earliest records, the Highlander was seen as backward and scary' is a reference to the earlier section of the passage where the writer has been setting out perceptions of the Highlander as primitive and savage **[1]**. The phrase 'a feeling fuelled more by fear than by superiority' introduces the idea that 'those of us

sweating away in polluted cities' should not feel superior since the way of life in the Highlands of the 21st century is of a high quality **[1]**.

6. Possible answers include:
   The parenthetical clause in lines 48–49 gives the reader additional information about what is meant by 'ecologically stressed age'. This is a reference to those not living in the Highlands. Within the parenthesis is a list of those problems facing the rest of us, making the Highlands appear more attractive **[2]**.
   The questions – 'Want to build an extension?', 'Need to get a turbine whirling?' – are written informally, which makes them appear casual and chatty and shows that some lifestyle concerns of urban dwellers are easily dealt with in the Highlands **[2]**.
   The answers to the questions are also written informally **[1]**, making a positive virtue of Highland living **[1]**.

7. The two short sentences in the final paragraph are memorable and forceful, making the paragraph an effective conclusion **[1]**. The first sentence refers back to the ideas earlier in the passage where the writer deals with how Lowlanders perceive Highlanders, while the second sentence – 'I prefer the word smart' – refers to the later part of the passage where she argues that Highlanders are astute **[1]**.

8. Possible answers include:

   Key idea 1
   The desolation of the battleground and the failure of Charlie's army.
   Passage 3
   The battleground is described as bleak, featureless and dismal, not least because of the defeat and collapse of the Jacobite army and the suffering of any survivors.
   Passage 4
   The battleground was a bleak moor, where in a gale of sleet and snow the Jacobites were ignominiously defeated by the superior Duke of Cumberland's army.

   Key idea 2
   The appearance and fighting ability of the Highlanders.
   Passage 3
   The Highlanders appeared as almost a caricature of themselves: ill-equipped and outnumbered, with meagre muskets and swords to fight an army that had cannon.
   Passage 4
   There were fewer than five thousand Highlanders, largely clansmen, hungry and exhausted, facing nine thousand well-equipped foot soldiers, militia man and artillery.

   Key idea 3
   The feelings of superiority shown by non-Highlanders.
   Passage 3
   Highlanders have been seen through the centuries as backward and terrifying in appearance and behaviour, making city dwellers feel superior to them.
   Passage 4
   Highlanders were treated appallingly by the victors and government after Culloden. The structure of the clan system was dismantled and allowed to atrophy, and the wearing of Highland dress was prohibited by the government.

Acknowledgements

The author and publisher are grateful to the copyright holders for permission to use quoted materials and images.

Pages 5-7, 'How to Build a Time Machine', Stephen Hawking, 2010 © Solo Syndication; Pages 8-9, 'The Big Question: Is time travel possible, and is there any chance that it will ever take place?', Steve Conor, 2008 © ESI Media syndication; Page 12, 'The fascinating hidden history of London's lost rivers', Tom Bolton, 2018 © Telegraph Media Group Limited 2018; Pages 14, 26 'Missing penalty not end of world but a chance to learn more about life', Matthew Syed, 2014 © The Times / News Licensing; Page 15, 'Can Britain afford to keep talented immigrants out?', Ruth Wishart, 2002 © Newsquest (Herald & Times) Ltd; Page 16, 'Cities on the Edge of Chaos', Deyan Sudjic, 2008 © Guardian News and Media Ltd 2018; Pages 18, 40, 'We must dare to dream but life is too precious to be derailed by failure', Matthew Syed © The Times / News Licensing; Page 19, 'The Importance of James Bond & Other Essays', Jef Costello, Edited by Greg Johnson © 2018 Counter-Currents Publishing, Ltd. Pages 20-21, 37, 41, 'Goodbye birds. Goodbye butterflies. Hello... farmageddon', Isabel Oakeshott, 2014 © The Times / News Licensing; Page 23, 'War on the car', Rob Edwards, 2010 © Newsquest (Herald & Times) Ltd; Pages 23, 37, extract © Ian Wooldridge, 2000; Pages 24(t), 33, 41, 43 'Addicted to shopping', Carol Midgley, 2009 © The Times / News Licensing; Page 24 (b), 'Want to exercise your mind? Try Playstation', Steven Johnson, 2005 © The Times / News Licensing; Page 25, 'Why do cats love bookstores?', Jason Diamond, 2016 © LITHUB; Pages 26-27, 'Paranoid parenting is the greatest danger to our kids', Melanie Reid, 2001 © Newsquest (Herald & Times) Ltd; Page 28, IMPACT! THE THREAT OF COMETS AND ASTEROIDS by Verschuur (1997) By Permission of Oxford University Press, USA.; Page 29, Marrakech by George Orwell (Copyright © George Orwell, 1938); Page 30, I'm A Little Special: A Muhammad Ali Reader © 1988 Gerald Early; Page 30, Shooting an Elephant by George Orwell (Copyright © George Orwell, 1946). Reprinted by permission of Bill Hamilton as the Literary Executor of the Estate of the Late Sonia Brownell Orwell. Pages 31, 39, Surviving the Shipwreck © Literary estate of William McIlvanney; Page 32, How to be a bad birdwatcher © 2004 Simon Barnes. Reprinted by kind permission of Short Books; Pages 33, 36, 'Rude, impulsive, sulky... still, let our 16-year-olds-vote', Catherine Bennett, 2012 © Guardian News and Media Ltd 2018. Pages 34, 35, 'Cutting down a tree is worse than fox hunng', Janice Turner, 2013 © The Times / News Licensing; Pages 36, 'Boris Johnson and our brilliantly hands-off parents', Rachel Johnson, 2012 © The Times / News Licensing; Page 38, 'Asteroid Could Blast Us Back To Dark Ages' © Jay Tate, The Spaceguard Centre; Page 42, 'Will Self: Is there nowhere I can escape the tyranny of muzak?', Will Self, 2012 © New Statesman Media; Page 44 Social media's outrage mob are only interested in one cause: themselves, Angela Haggerty © Newsquest (Herald & Times) Ltd; Page 45, 'Back off! ... Now hipster foodies are coming for our porridge', Karen Goodwin 2009 © Newsquest (Herald & Times) Ltd; Pages 54-55, 'Forget Culloden: today's Highlanders have it made', Rosemary Goring, 2009 © Newsquest (Herald & Times) Ltd; Pages 56-57, The Lion in the North © 1981 John Prebble; Page 68, 'Can the Frozen star Idina Menzel ever let go of Let it Go?', Ed Potton, 2015 © The Times / News Licensing

Every effort has been made to trace copyright holders and obtain their permission for the use of copyright material. The author and publisher will gladly receive information enabling them to rectify any error or omission in subsequent editions. All facts are correct at time of going to press.

Published by Collins
An imprint of HarperCollinsPublishers
1 London Bridge Street,
London, SE1 9GF

© HarperCollinsPublishers Limited 2018

9780008306663

First published 2018

10 9 8 7 6 5 4 3 2 1

British Library Cataloguing in Publication Data.

A CIP record of this book is available from the British Library.

Printed in United Kingdom.

Commissioning Editor: Gillian Bowman
Project manager: Rachel Allegro
Author: David Cockburn
Proofreader: Jess White
Copy editor: Louise Robb
Project management: Project One Publishing Solutions, Scotland
Typesetting: Jouve
Cover designers: Kneath Associates and Sarah Duxbury
Production: Natalia Rebow

From the author:
I should like to pay tribute to Leckie and Leckie's highly talented team, whose support and understanding goes beyond expectation. And I should like to thank Kevin Cockburn without whose endless encouragement and patience this book would never have been written.